FIRST PETER
In the Greek New Testament

Price One Dollar per Volume

FIRST PETER

In the Greek New Testament

for

The English Reader

by

KENNETH S. WUEST

Teacher of New Testament Greek
at the
Moody Bible Institute of Chicago

SECOND EDITION

WM. B. EERDMANS PUBLISHING COMPANY
Grand Rapids   1944   Mich., U.S.A.

FIRST PETER IN THE GREEK NEW TESTAMENT
by KENNETH S. WUEST

DEDICATED

To my beloved wife, Jeannette Irene Wuest, brave soldier of the Cross full of faith and good works, my companion in life, my diligent and self-sacrificing co-worker in the ministry of the Word, the one who spurs me on to the highest endeavors, my wise counselor, my comforter in hours of stress and strain, my God-given helpmeet whose consistent and sweet Christian life is ever a blessing and help to me.

INTRODUCTION

This is no book to peruse in one's easy chair. It is designed, like its predecessor, *Philippians in the Greek New Testament*, for use on the Christian's study table alongside of his Bible. The book is a simplified Greek commentary making available to the Bible student who is not acquainted with Greek, and who has had no formal training in Bible study, a wealth of informative and explanatory material that will throw a flood of light upon his English Bible. The translation offered is what might be called a fuller translation, using more words than a standard version of the Scriptures in order to bring out more of the richness of the Greek, and make certain passages clearer, where the condensed literality of the standard translations tends to obscure their meaning. Words in parenthesis are not part of the translation but are explanatory. The translation must not be used as a substitute for, but as a companion to the standard translation the student is using.

The writer has confined himself largely to interpretation. The fundamental basis of all Christian life and service is a clear understanding of what the Word of God means. This is what the word studies and the fuller translation seek to give the Bible student. While devotional studies where the truth is applied to Christian life and service are most helpful and desirable, yet it is a good thing for the Christian to do some study for himself also. The Bible student can study First Peter, verse by verse, with the help of the word studies and the fuller translation, developing the truth and applying it to his own life. The Holy Spirit, if recognized and depended upon for His teaching ministry, will lead the earnest Christian into such fresh, new truth that this study will be one succession of spiritual discoveries and thrills.

The book is not written for the scholar, and lays no claim to being a finished piece of work on the Greek text of First Peter. It is designed for those who love the Lord and His Word and delight in feasting upon it. The eighteen units into which it is divided can be used as a basis for a series of Bible expositions or expository sermons. The index makes it possible for the student to turn quickly to any verse desired. Where a word is treated more fully or in its every New Testament occurrence in the author's other books, a footnote will direct the reader to the page or pages where that treatment may be found. The English translation referred to is the Authorized Version.

K. S. W.

CONTENTS

FIRST PETER
In the Greek New Testament

1.

THREE STEPS IN A SINNER'S SALVATION (1:1, 2)

Verse one

THE inspired writer of this letter, whose original name was Simon, received the Aramaic name of Cephas as a descriptive title of what he would some day be like (John 1:42). The A. V. translates, "Thou shalt be called Cephas, which is by interpretation, a stone." The word "stone" is from the Greek word *petros* which means "a detached but large fragment of rock," and is used here metaphorically to describe Peter as a man like a rock by reason of his firmness and strength of soul. The name "Peter" is the English spelling of the Greek *petros* which is the word chosen by the Holy Spirit that would adequately translate the meaning of the Aramaic "Cephas." In answering Peter's great confession of His deity, the Lord Jesus says, "Thou art Peter (*petros*), and upon this rock (*petra*) I will build my church" (Matt. 16:18). Thayer quotes Schmidt as treating *petros* and *petra* as synonyms, *petros* meaning "a detached but large fragment of rock," *petra* "the massive living rock." The foundation of the Church of Jesus Christ is that massive living rock, the Son of God seen in His deity, acknowledged as such by Peter. Peter is but a fragment of that massive rock in the sense in which he speaks of believers as "lively stones," deriving their eternal life from the great Living Stone Himself (2:4, 5.) It was the fulness of the Holy Spirit at Pentecost that transformed Simon into Peter, the Rock-Man.

He designates himself as an apostle, the word "apostle" coming from *apostolos* made up of *apo*, "off," and *stello*, "to send," a technical word used of one sent from someone else

with credentials on a mission. Peter was an ambassador of
Jesus Christ sent by Him with credentials in the form of miracles, and on a mission, that of proclaiming the good news of
salvation. Those to whom he writes, he designates as strangers.
The English word "strangers" refers to anyone with whom we
are not acquainted. But the Greek word means far more than
that. It is *parepidemois,* made up of *para,* "alongside of,"
epi, "upon," and *demos,* used in Biblical Greek of the people of a heathen city. The word here describes the recipients
of this letter as Christians who have settled down alongside
of the unsaved. Peter uses the same word in 2:11. He will
not let us forget that we are living among the unsaved who
are always carefully observing us.

The word "scattered" is from *diasporas.* This word is found
in the LXX[1] where Moses says of Israel, "Thou shalt be removed into all the kingdoms of the earth" (Deut. 28:25), and
is probably the earliest example of its use as a technical designation of the Jews who for whatever reason lived outside of
Palestine. The word is used in John 7:35 and James 1:1, in
both places referring to those Jews who were living outside of
Palestine. Peter uses it in the same way. We thus see that the
recipients of this letter were Christian Jews. These Jews were
living among the Gentiles in the various provinces named by
Peter, all of which were in Asia Minor.

The word *diaspora* is the noun form of *diaspeiro,* which
verb is made up of *dia,* "through" and *speiro,* "to sow, to
scatter seed," which latter is the derivative from which *sperma*
the Greek word for "seed" comes. This scattering of these
Jews referred to in First Peter took place previous to the
world-wide dispersion, A.D. 70, which latter was the judgment
of God upon the apostasy of Israel. The great majority of the
Jews living outside of Palestine in the first century and before
A.D. 70, were living where they were by their own choice, the
chief reason being the opportunity for business activity which
the Gentile centers of population afforded. There they were

---

1. *The Greek Translation of the Old Testament.*

when the Christian missionaries contacted them. There they had been providentially sown by the great Sower, to become themselves disseminators of the gospel story. The application can be made to all Christians. We who are saved, are providentially placed by God in the midst of the unsaved, living in Satan's territory, for he is the god of the world system, to win those among whom we have been placed, to the Lord Jesus.

Verse two

The recipients of this letter are called "elect." The word is *eklektois*, a plural adjective from the verb *eklego* which means "to pick out" or "to select out of a number." The verb is used in Ephesians 1:4 where it is rendered "chosen," referring to the act of God in sovereign grace choosing out certain from among mankind for Himself, the verb in Ephesians being middle in voice, speaking of the subject acting in his own interest. These to whom Peter is writing are "selected out ones." The words "according to" are the translation of *kata* whose root meaning is "down," which gives the idea of domination. This choice out from a number was dominated by the foreknowledge of God the Father. This is the first step in the act of God bringing a sinner into the place of salvation. God the Father chooses him out, this choice being dominated or controlled or determined by His foreknowledge.

The word "foreknowledge" is the translation of the noun *prognosin* which is found twice in the New Testament, its verb form *proginosko*, five times. In Acts 26:5 and II Peter 3:17 we have the purely classical meaning of the verb, namely, "previous knowledge." But in Acts 2:23, and I Peter 1:2, the meaning of the noun form, and in Romans 8:29 and 11:2, and I Peter 1:20, the meaning of the verb form, goes beyond the purely classical meaning of the possession of previous knowledge, and refers to that which the A.V. in I Peter 1:20 calls foreordination. The first time the noun form *prognosin* is found is in Acts 2:23, where it is used in the clause, "him being delivered by the determinate counsel and foreknowledge of God." The words "counsel" and "foreknowledge" are in a Greek construction which makes both words refer here to the same act, presenting that act in its two aspects. The content of meaning in the word "foreknowledge" here is made clear therefore by the words "the determinate counsel." The meaning of "foreknowledge" here and in the other four places where the words "foreknew" and "foreknowledge" occur, cannot be merely "previous knowledge." The Greek word "counsel," *boule,* refers to an interchange of opinions, a mutual advising, the exchange of deliberative judgment. The word "determinate" is the translation of *horismenei,* a perfect participle which refers to the past act of putting limits upon something with the present result that some certain thing has been appointed or decreed. The word "foreknowledge" therefore refers to that counsel of God in which after deliberative judgment, the Lord Jesus was to be delivered into human hands to be crucified. In I Peter 1:20, He is the One who was foreordained before the foundation of the world to be the Lamb who was to take away the sins of lost humanity. Thus, in I Peter 1:2, the word "foreknowledge" refers to that counsel of God in which after deliberative judgment certain from among mankind were designated to a certain position, that position being defined by the context.

The second step in the salvation of a sinner is seen in the words "through sanctification of the Spirit unto obedience." The Greek makes it clear that it is the Holy Spirit who does the sanctifying. The Greek word "sanctify" means "to set apart." The word "through" is the translation of *en,* which means literally "in." The whole phrase is in a grammatical classification known as the locative of sphere. It was in the sphere of the setting apart work of the Spirit that the sinner was chosen. That is, God the Father chose the sinner out from among mankind to be the recipient of the setting-apart work of the Spirit, in which work the Holy Spirit sets the sinner apart from his unbelief to the act of faith in the Lord Jesus. The act of faith is spoken of here by the word "obedi-

ence," which is not the obedience of the saint, but that of the
sinner to the Faith, for this act is answered by his being
cleansed in the precious blood of Jesus. In Acts 6:7 we read
that "a great company of the priests were obedient to the
faith." Thus, the second step in the salvation of a sinner is
taken by the Holy Spirit who brings the one chosen to the
act of faith in the Lord Jesus as Saviour.

This is followed by the third step in which God the Son
cleanses that believing sinner in His precious blood. This is
given us in the words "sprinkling of the blood of Jesus
Christ," Peter using the phraseology and typology of the Levitical ritual where the priest sprinkled the people with the sac-
rificial blood (Heb. 9:19).

We have therefore the three steps taken by the three Persons of the Triune God. God the Father chooses the sinner to
salvation. God the Spirit brings the sinner thus chosen to the
act of faith. God the Son cleanses him in His precious blood.
Perhaps someone may read these lines who is not saved. Your
question is, "How can I know whether I am one of those
whom God has chosen?" The answer is simple. Put your
faith in the Lord Jesus as your personal Saviour, the One who
died on the Cross in your stead to make atonement for your
sins, and God will save you. You will find that God the Father chose you for salvation, God the Spirit brought you to the
act of faith, and God the Son cleansed you from your sin.

The Greek word "grace" is so rich in its meaning that the
reader is referred to the author's other books for a study of its
classical and New Testament meanings, where it is fully
treated.[1] Here the word refers to the enabling grace for daily
Christian living which is given to the saint yielded to and dependent upon the Holy Spirit. The peace spoken of here is
not justifying peace, but peace of heart produced by the Holy
Spirit in the heart of the Spirit-filled saint.

---

1. *Treasures*, pp. 15-19.

FULLER TRANSLATION

(1) *Peter, an ambassador of Jesus Christ, to those who have settled down alongside of the native pagan population, scattered as seed throughout Pontus, Galatia, Cappadocia, Asia, and Bithynia, (2) chosen-out ones, this choice having been determined by the foreordination of God the Father, those chosen out to be recipients of the setting-apart work of the Spirit resulting in obedience (of faith) and (thus) in the sprinkling of the blood of Jesus Christ. Grace (be) to you, and (heart) peace be multiplied.*

2.

THE SAINT'S INHERITANCE (1:3-5)

Verse three

THE mention of God in verse two is followed by the Benediction of the Name, as Jewish piety prescribed. God the Father is the central figure in verses 3-5, God the Son, in verses 6-9, and God the Holy Spirit, in verses 10-12. The word "blessed" is the translation of *eulogetos* from which we get our words "eulogize" and "eulogy." The Greek word means "to praise, to celebrate with praises." The word is a compound of *eu* which means "well" and is used in such expressions as "well done" or "to do well," and *logeo* which has the same root as *logos,*" a word," and is associated with *lego,* "to speak." Thus, the word means "to bless" someone in the sense of speaking well of him. Another Greek word, *makarios,* meaning in secular Greek "prosperous" and in the New Testament "spiritually prosperous," the idea of "spiritually" coming from its usage in its context, is found in Matthew 5:3-11. That is, the meek are spiritually prosperous. Our Lord said, "There is more spiritual prosperity in the act of constantly giving than in the act of constantly receiving" (Acts 20:35). All of which goes to say that a Christian grows faster spiritually by giving sacrificially of himself in the Lord's service than in receiving the spiritual ministrations of others. The latter is perfectly proper and is needed, but a sponge-like absorption alone is not conducive to a healthy growth in the Christian life. Christian character is developed, not by one's knowledge of the Word of God, but by putting into practice what one knows of the Word of God. Spiritual prosperity is not dependent upon what one takes in of the Word, but upon what one gives out of himself in the service of the Lord Jesus as one obeys the Word.

The word Peter uses (*eulogetos*) is one in which he blesses God in the sense that he eulogizes, speaks well of, praises Him. Peter, a Jew with an Old Testament Jewish background, writing to Christian Jews of the same background, speaks of the God of Israel as the "God and Father of our Lord Jesus Christ," thus recognizing the latter in His human relationship to God the Father, for our Lord in His incarnate humanity worshipped God and recognized Him as His Father. Yet he also takes into account His deity in the name "Jesus" which means "Jehovah-Saviour," and also in the name "Christ" which means "the Anointed One."

The word "which" is from a masculine article in the Greek text, and should therefore be rendered "who," referring as it does to God who is a person. "According to" is from *kata* whose root meaning is "down." From this we get the idea of domination, thus not "according to the measure of His abundant mercy," but "impelled by His abundant mercy." It was the compelling constraint in the merciful heart of God that made inevitable the atonement for sinners.

"Hath begotten" is from an aorist participle, and refers merely to the past fact of begetting, "begat us." "Again" is from the preposition *ana* prefixed to the participle, the preposition meaning in composition with another word, "renewal, new again." Thus, regeneration is spoken of here, the act of the Holy Spirit imparting to us a new life, making us partakers of the divine nature and thus children of God, a begetting anew. The word "unto" is from *eis*, a preposition speaking of result in this context. Alford translates "so that we have." The hope here is not only an objective thing, but a subjective hope on the part of the believer. It is a lively hope, that is, not only living, but actively alive, an energizing principle of divine life in the believer, a Christian hopefulness and optimism produced in the believer yielded to the indwelling Holy Spirit. It is both an attitude of expectancy as the Christian looks forward to the inheritance awaiting him in heaven, and a hopefulness of present blessing from God in this life in view of the eternal blessedness of the believer in the next life. A child of God has no right to look on the dark side of things, and to look for the worst to happen to him. As the object of God's care and love, he has the right to look for the best to come to him and to look on the bright side of things. "The path of the just is as the shining light that shineth more and more unto the perfect day. The way of the wicked is as darkness: they know not at what they stumble" (Prov. 4:18, 19).

This lively hope is made possible by the resurrection of the Lord Jesus in that it is through the believer's identification with Him in the resurrection that he is given a new life in regeneration, and thus will also be able to enjoy the heavenly inheritance into which he has been born. The word "from" is not from *apo* which means "from the edge of," but from *ek* which means "out from within." Our Lord was raised out from among the rest of the dead. He as the Man Christ Jesus went to the part of Hades reserved for the righteous dead, and His body lay in Joseph's tomb. But when He was raised from the dead, the rest of those in Hades stayed there, and their bodies remained in the earth. But He left that place, and reunited with His body glorified, appeared alive again after three days. That is what the expression "out from among the dead" means.

Verse four

As begotten children of God, we become His heirs, and joint-heirs with His Son Jesus Christ (Rom. 8:17), and thus come into an inheritance. This inheritance is incorruptible because it belongs to the future life which the risen saints share with God Himself. It is undefiled as our great High Priest is undefiled (Heb. 7:26 same word). It is non-fading, not able to wither away, as a flower would. The word "reserved" is from *tereo* which means "to watch, to observe, to guard, protect, to reserve, set aside." Heaven is the safe-deposit box where God is guarding our inheritance for us under constant surveillance. The participle is in the perfect tense, speaking of a past completed action having present results. We could translate, "has been laid up and is now kept guarded in safe deposit."

Verse five

"Kept" is from *phrouomenous,* a present participle implying action constantly going on. It is a military term, meaning "to guard or protect." Illustrations of its use in secular documents are given by Moulton and Milligan in their *Vocabulary of the Greek Testament*: "belonging to the guard at Socnopaei Nesus," "at Kerkeosiris, which is unguarded and not situated upon the great river." While our inheritance is being kept guarded in heaven under the watchful eye of God, we are being garrisoned about by God's protecting care for it. The guard is never changed. It is on duty twenty-four hours a day, year in and year out until we arrive safe in heaven.

This protection is God's response to our faith which we exercised in the Lord Jesus as Saviour and which now rests in Him as our Preserver. Our faith lays hold of this power, and this power strengthens our faith, and thus we are preserved. The salvation spoken of here is of course the glorification of our bodies. We received our justification at the moment we believed. We are receiving our sanctification, namely victory over sin and growth in the Christian life now. We will yet receive that part of salvation which awaits us in Glory.

FULLER TRANSLATION

(3) *Let the God and Father of our Lord Jesus Christ be eulogized, who impelled by His abundant mercy begat us anew so that we have a lively hope, this lively hope having*

*been made actual through the intermediate instrumentality
of the resurrection of Jesus Christ out from among those who
are dead, (4) and an inheritance incorruptible, and undefiled, and that does not fade away, which inheritance has been
laid up and is now kept guarded in safe deposit in heaven for
you, (5) who are constantly being kept guarded by the power
of God through faith for a salvation ready to be revealed in
the last time.*

3.

THE PURPOSE OF CHRISTIAN SUFFERING (1:6-9)

Verse six

THE word "wherein" is most naturally referred by the English reader to the word "salvation" in verse 5. It is true that we rejoice in our salvation. But here the Greek text helps us to the correct interpretation, for the word goes back to "time," since the Greek word "salvation" is feminine in gender and the word "time" is neuter, the word "wherein" being neuter, referring back to its neuter antecedent. Herein lies the value of the Greek. The rules of Greek grammar are just as clear and definite as those of mathematics. It is as simple a matter as that of fitting a round peg in a round hole, and a square peg in a square hole. The saints are to rejoice in the last time, that is, when they receive their glorified bodies at the Rapture. "Rejoice" is from a Greek word speaking of extreme joy expressing itself externally in an exuberant triumph of joy. In verse 8 we see that it is a glorified joy made possible by our future glorified state, a joy not possible now in our mortal bodies. Tears of joy are just an evidence of the inability of our present state to fully feel the joy that comes to us at times. But then in our bodies of glory we will be able to drink in and appreciate all the boundless joys of the Saviour's presence.

"Season" is from *oligon* which means "little, small, few," and refers here to a little while. Surely, this present life is a little while compared to eternity. And then a loving God sees to it that in the midst of the shadows and heartaches and trials, His children have their days of sunshine even in this life. The words "if need be" are hypothetical, not affirmative.

That is, they do not state that there is always a need for the dark days, for testing times and difficulties. In some lives there seems to be more need of trials than in others. To those servants of God whom He purposes to use in a larger, greater way, many trials are allowed to come, for "we must be ground between the millstones of suffering before we can be bread for the multitude." And then, in the case of a saint who is not living close to his Lord, it is necessary to send disciplinary trials to purge his life of sin and draw him into a closer walk with God.

The words "ye are in heaviness" could be rendered "ye have been made sorrowful." The word "temptations" is from *peirasmos* which refers both to trials and testings, and also solicitations to do evil, in short, to all that goes to furnish a test of character. The trials may come from God or under His permissive will from Satan, or may be the result of our own wrong doing. The solicitations to do evil come from the world, the evil nature, or Satan. These are described as manifold, namely, variegated. The word emphasizes the diversity rather than the number of the trials. The word "through" is from *en* with the locative, speaking of the sphere in which these Christians have been made sorrowful.

Verse seven

In this verse we are informed as to the reason and purpose of these trials, namely, that the trial of our faith might result in praise and honor and glory at the appearing of Jesus Christ. The word "trial" is the translation of *dokimion* the noun, *dokimazo* being the verb of the same root, the latter referring to the act of putting someone or something to the test with a view of determining whether it is worthy of being approved or not, the test being made with the intention of approving if possible. The word was used of the act of examining candidates for the degree of Doctor of Medicine. It is the approval of our faith which is to resound to the praise of the Lord Jesus. Testing times put our faith to the test, and as we are

submissive to God and remain faithful to Him and are ready
to have Him teach us the lessons He would have us learn
through them, we demonstrate by our actions that the faith
we have is a genuine God-given, Holy Spirit produced faith,
the genuine article. This faith and its working in our lives
is to the glory of the Lord Jesus. It is not the testing of our
faith that is to the glory of God, but the fact that our faith
has met the test and has been approved, that redounds to His
glory. This is made very clear by the Greek grammar involved in the statement.

It is not the approved faith, but the approval itself that is
in the apostle's mind here. For instance, a gold-mining company wishes to buy a proposed site where gold is said to have
been found. But it is not sure whether the metal is real gold
or not and whether it is there in sufficient quantity so that a
mine if sunk would be a profitable venture. It engages an
assayer of metals to take samples of the gold ore to his labora-
tory and examine them. The assayer sends his report to the
effect that the ore contains true gold, and that the gold is
found in sufficient quantity so that the venture will pay. The
report of the assayer approving the gold ore is of far more
value to the mining company than the gold he returns with his
report, for upon the basis of the report, the company can go
ahead with assurance and buy the land and begin mining op-
erations. The fact that God finds our faith to be one which
He can approve, is of far more value to Him and to His glory,
than the approved faith, for He has something to work with,
a faith that He knows can stand the testings and the trials
which may come to the Christian. The fact that God can
trust a Christian as one that is dependable, is of great value
to Him. God is looking for faithful, dependable workers, not
necessarily gifted, educated, cultured ones. It is a "well done,
thou good and faithful servant" that will greet the ears of the
saint at the Judgment Seat of Christ.

Peter tells us that this approval of our faith is much more
precious than the approval of gold, even though that gold be

approved through fire-testing. The words "of gold" of the A.V. are an excellent rendering for a literal word-for-word translation. But the words "the approval of" are necessarily supplied to make clear the apostle's thought. It is not the approval of our faith that is compared to gold, but to the approval of gold. The picture here is of an ancient gold-smith who puts his crude gold ore in a crucible, subjects it to intense heat, and thus liquifies the mass. The impurities rise to the surface and are skimmed off. When the metal-worker is able to see the reflection of his face clearly mirrored in the surface of the liquid, he takes it off the fire, for he knows that the contents are pure gold. So it is with God and His child. He puts us in the crucible of Christian suffering, in which process sin is gradually put out of our lives, our faith is purified from the slag of unbelief that somehow mingles with it so often, and the result is the reflection of the face of Jesus Christ in the character of the Christian. This, above all, God the Father desires to see. Christlikeness is God's ideal for His child. Christian suffering is one of the most potent means to that end.

Verses eight and nine

The Christians to whom Peter was writing were not personal disciples of Jesus, but converts of the apostles. They had not seen the Lord Jesus on earth during His incarnate residence here, either while in His humiliation or at the time of His post-resurrection ministry. The Greek has it, "Of whom not having had a glimpse." Yet they loved Him. They never saw the Lord Jesus with the physical sense of sight, but ah, what a vivid portrait of Him did the Holy Spirit paint for them on the canvas of their spiritual vision. And that is the perfectly proper order for this Age of Grace. Paul says "Though we have known Christ after the flesh, yet now henceforth know we him no more" (II Cor. 5:16). The picture of the earthly Lord Jesus in His mortal body, seen by human eyes, is supplanted now by the picture of the glorified Man in

the Glory, painted by the Holy Spirit for the spiritual vision
of the saint. The poet[1] sings, "I read thy Word, O Lord, each
passing day, and in the sacred page find glad employ: But this
I pray — Save from the killing letter. Teach my heart, *set free
from human forms*,[2] the holy art of reading thee in every line,
in precept, prophecy, and sign, till, all my vision filled with
thee, thy likeness shall reflect in me. Not knowledge but thyself my joy! — For this I pray." It is as we free ourselves from
the conception an artist may have of what he thinks the Lord
Jesus looked like in His life on earth, and depend upon the
Holy Spirit through the Word to reveal to us the likeness of
our Lord Jesus, that we come to some true conception of Him
in His glorified state. We will recognize Him in the Glory
over yonder, not by what human artists have conceived Him
to be, but by the Holy Spirit's portrait of Him.

These saints loved the Lord Jesus, even though they had
never had a glimpse of Him with their physical sense of sight.
But one cannot love another unless one has some clear-cut
conception of that person. One must know the person in order
to love him. It was the clear-cut conception of the Lord Jesus
which the Holy Spirit had given these saints through the
Word, that caused them to love Him. The distinctive Greek
word for "love" here, *agape,* refers to a love that is called out
of one's heart by the preciousness of the person loved. But
even the preciousness of the Lord Jesus would not have made
these individuals love Him if God in salvation had not produced in them that divine love which He Himself is, with
which to love Him (Rom. 5:5; Gal. 5:22, 23). One must have
the nature of an artist to really appreciate and love art. One
must have the nature of God (II Peter 1:4) to appreciate and
love the Lord Jesus. It is this ideal combination of a study of
God's Word and a definite subjection to the Holy Spirit that
results in the clear, vivid portrait of the Lord Jesus in the spiritual vision of the saint. To know Him is to love Him. To
know Him better, is to love Him better. The secret of an in-

---

1. Rev. J. C. Macaulay in *Thyself.*
2. Italics ours.

timate, loving fellowship with the Lord Jesus, the secret of knowing Him in an intimate way, is in the moment-by-moment control of the Holy Spirit over the life of the Christian believer.

Then Peter draws the same contrast between the present sorrow and future joy of verse 6 in this verse, where he contrasts our present seeing Him with the eye of faith and our future seeing Him face to face at the Rapture, at which time we will rejoice with an unspeakable and glorified joy, and at which time we will receive the consummation of our faith, namely, the salvation of our souls, deliverance from the presence of sin in the glorification of our physical bodies.

FULLER TRANSLATION

(6) *In which last time you are to be constantly rejoicing with a joy that expresses itself in a triumphant exuberance, although for a little while at the present time if perchance there is need for it, you have been made sorrowful in the midst of many different kinds of testings,* (7) *in order that the approval of your faith, which faith was examined by testing for the purpose of being approved, that approval being much more precious than the approval of gold which perishes, even though that gold be approved by fire-testing, may be discovered after scrutiny to result in praise and glory and honor at the time of the revelation of Jesus Christ;* (8) *of whom not having had a glimpse, you love because of His preciousness, in whom, now not seeing, yet believing, you are to be rejoicing with an inexpressible and glorified joy,* (9) *upon the occasion of your receiving the promised consummation of your faith which is the (final) salvation of your souls.*

4.

THE SILENCE OF THE OLD TESTAMENT
REGARDING THE BODY OF CHRIST (1:10-12)

Verses ten to twelve

THE mention of their salvation in verse 9, leads the apostle to relate the same to the Old Testament writers for the information of the Jewish recipients of his letter. There is no article before "prophets" in the Greek text. It was the Old Testament prophets as a class of individuals that conducted an exhaustive inquiry and search into their own writings. Peter speaks of this grace which they wrote about as "the particular grace destined for you" (Greek), inferring that believers in this age have something unique and for them alone. What they looked for was as to *what time* or if they could not find that, *what kind of time* would usher in this particular unique salvation. The answer to their question would throw light upon the character of that salvation. There are two words referring to time, *chronos* which speaks of time contemplated simply as such, the succession of moments, and *kairos* which speaks of a limited period of time, with the added notion of suitableness. Both words appear in the answer of Jesus, "It is not for you to know the times or the seasons" (Acts 1:6, 7), the times (*chronos*), the seasons (*kairos*). The seasons (*kairos*) are the joints or articulations of the times (*chronos*). The seasons (*kairos*) represent the critical epoch-making periods when all that has been maturing through long ages comes to a head in grand decisive events which constitute the close of one period and the beginning of another. Such an event the prophets were searching for. If they could find out when it would occur, well and good, and if not, they would attempt to ascertain of what character the event would be.

Their inquiry was regarding the relation of this event as to order in time or with respect to the economy of God, to the atonement of our Lord at the Cross and His future glorious reign in the Millennial Kingdom. They searched the Old Testament scriptures as to what the Holy Spirit, who was in them when they wrote their inspired books, was pointing to or making plain when He bore testimony to the sufferings and the glory of the Lord Jesus. It was revealed to them that this truth concerning the particular grace that was destined for believers of this age, was not for them but for those of this dispensation.

The great event ushering in a new order of things which they were looking for was Pentecost, the time when the Body of Christ was formed. Paul speaks of this mystery in the words, "which in other ages was not made known unto the sons of men, as it is now revealed unto his holy apostles and prophets by the Spirit; that the Gentiles should be fellow-heirs, and of the same body, and partakers of his promise in Christ by the gospel" (Eph. 3:5, 6). That the Gentiles were to be saved, was no mystery to the Old Testament writers, but that the wall of separation so rigidly held in Old Testament times between Gentile and Jew was to be broken down at the Cross, and that the two would become one body, that was the mystery. Peter did not see this truth until eight years after Pentecost (Acts 10:1-48). Here we have the great truth of the Body of Christ, its living Head, the Lord Jesus Himself, its members, all believers of this Age of Grace which began at Pentecost and closes with the Rapture, Jew and Gentile becoming one body in Christ.

Peter says that the angels desire to look into these things. The word "desire" is a strong one, referring to a passionate desire. "To look into" is the translation of *parakupto*, used in Luke 24:12 and John 20:5, 11, of Peter, John, and Mary stooping down and looking into the empty tomb. The word means, "to look at with head bent forward, to look into with the body bent, to stoop and look into." Metaphorically it means, "to look carefully into, to inspect curiously." It is used in the latter sense in this passage. The preposition *para* prefixed to the verb means "beside" and is used at times with a case denoting separation. Thus the angels peer into the mysteries of Church truth from beside it, like the cherubim bending over the Mercy Seat where man has access to God through a substitutionary sacrifice that cleanses him from sin. They are not participants in the salvation but spectators of it. Paul writing in a context of this mystery says, "To the intent that now unto the principalities and powers in heavenly places might be known by the church the manifold wisdom of God" (Eph. 3:10). The principalities and powers are of course the holy angels. The manifold wisdom of God as seen in the context is the truth of the Body of Christ. "Might be known" is passive and is more properly rendered "might be made known." "By" is the translation of *dia*, the preposition of immediate agency. That is, this truth is to be made known to the holy angels by means of the instrumentality of the Church. The Church is the teacher of angels. Paul says that the apostles "are made a spectacle unto the world, and to angels, and to men" (I Cor. 4:9). How the angels watch the saints. How they wonder at creatures once totally depraved, now living holy lives that glorify God. It is in the Church that they catch the supreme view of God's love, sinners saved by grace, raised to a seat in the heavenly places in Christ. The Church is God's university for angels. The verse reads, "To the intent that now to the principalities and powers in heavenly places might be made known by means of the instrumentality of the church, the manifold wisdom of God."

FULLER TRANSLATION

(10) *Concerning which salvation prophets conducted an exhaustive inquiry and search, those who prophesied concerning the particular grace destined for you,* (11) *searching as to what season or character of season the Spirit of Christ who was in them was making plain, when He[1] was testifying beforehand concerning the sufferings of Christ and the glories which would come after these sufferings,* (12) *to whom it was revealed that not for themselves were they ministering these things which now have been reported to you through those who have announced the glad tidings to you by the Holy Spirit who was sent down on a commission from heaven, into which things the angels have a passionate desire to look carefully.*

---

1. *Riches,* pp. 117-120.

5.

THE HOLY WALK OF THE BELIEVER (1:13-16)

Verse thirteen

THE "wherefore" is equivalent to, "in view of the fact that even though you are undergoing many kinds of trials (v. 6), yet because your heavenly inheritance awaits you" (vv.3-6), gird up the loins of your minds. Peter here uses an oriental expression referring to the act of gathering up around the waist, the long, loose eastern robes which would impede one's progress in running or other exertion. The recipients of this letter are reminded by the apostle in 1:1 that they are strangers, those who have temporarily settled down alongside of a pagan population, and also pilgrims as well (2:11). As such they should always be ready to move. The Israelites had orders to eat the Passover with their loins girded, their shoes on their feet, their staff in their hand, ready to move on a moment's notice (Ex. 12:11).

It is not physical exertion that Peter has in mind here, but mental. If the purpose of girding up the clothing was to put out of the way that which would impede the physical progress of an individual, the girding up of the loins of the mind would be the putting out of the mind all that would impede the free action of the mind in connection with the onward progress of the Christian experience, things such as worry, fear, jealousy, hate, unforgiveness, impurity. These things harbored in the mind prevent the Holy Spirit from using the mental faculties of the Christian in the most efficient manner, and thus from causing that believer to grow in the Christian life and make progress in his salvation. The word "to gird up" is in the aorist tense which refers to a past once-for-all act. Bringing this oriental expression over to the occidental manner of thinking, enables us to translate, "Wherefore, having put out of the way, once for all, everything that would impede the free action of your mind." Peter treats this as a God-expected obligation on the part of the believer. In 1:3 we learned that as the believer definitely subjected himself to the ministry of the Holy Spirit, He would produce in his life through the Word, that Christian optimism that always looks for the best and not for the worst, that always sees the silver lining on every cloud. By the power of the same Holy Spirit, he is able to exert his will in putting out of his mind those things that would impede its free action. Thus, the Christian has the privilege of enjoying the wholesome mental atmosphere called "Christian optimism and a care-free mind," not a mind devoid of an appreciation of the seriousness of life and its responsibilities, but a mind not crippled and frozen by worry, fear, and their related mental attitudes. Living in this blessed mental state, the believer is ready and able to obey the exhortations to which the apostle now addresses himself.

The first one is, "be sober." The Greek word means, "to be calm and collected in spirit, to be temperate, dispassionate, circumspect." It speaks of the proper exercise of the mind, that state of mind in which the individual is self-controlled, and is able to see things without the distortion caused by worry, fear, and their related attitudes. The second admonition is, "hope to the end for the grace that is to be brought unto you at the revelation of Jesus Christ." The words, "hope to the end," do not refer to the Christian living in a state of hopefulness to the end of his life. The word "end" is the translation of *teleios*[1] which means "perfectly, completely." The root idea of the word refers to that which is in a state of completeness. Thus this adverb qualifies the verb "hope" and describes this hope. It is to be a hope that is complete, a perfect hope, wanting nothing, being in its

---

1. *Treasures*, pp. 113-121.

character an assured expectation. One could translate, "set your hope perfectly, unchangeably, without doubt and despondency."

Peter had spoken of the saint's inheritance which will be his in the last time (1:4, 5). Here he refers to this inheritance as the grace that will be his at the revelation of the Lord Jesus. The words "that is to be brought" are from an article and a present participle in the Greek text. It is true that our reception of this grace is yet future. But the picture in the word used is of this grace being brought to us right now. That is, it is already on the way. It is on the divine menu. We have our justification the moment we put our faith in the Lord Jesus. It is ours forever. We are having our sanctification during our earthly life, namely, the work of the Holy Spirit in our hearts giving us victory over sin and producing in us His fruit as we are definitely subjected to Him. We will have our glorification, namely, the transformation of our physical bodies at the Rapture. The first two courses on the divine menu, justification and sanctification, we are enjoying now. Peter exhorts us to set our hope perfectly, wholly, and unchangeably, without doubt and despondency upon our future glorification. It is like eating a bountiful repast at the home of Mrs. Charming Hostess. While we are enjoying the delicious meal, we are not worrying whether there will be dessert or not. We know it is on the menu, and is being brought to us as soon as we are ready for it. Alford translates "which is even now bearing down upon you." The word means literally "to carry." One could thus translate, "which is being brought to you."

Verse fourteen

The words "as obedient children" are literally in the Greek, "as children of obedience." The motive principal of the child of God should be obedience, the latter being related to him as a parent is to a child. As children inherit the nature of their parents, so a child of God is made a partaker of the divine nature, which nature always impels to the act of obedience. It is natural for a child of God to obey Him.

In our characters as obedient children of God, we are exhorted not to fashion ourselves with respect to our former lusts. The word "fashion"[1] in the Greek text refers to the act of assuming an outward appearance patterned after some certain thing, an appearance or expression which does not come from and is not representative of one's inmost and true nature. It refers here to the act of a child of God assuming as an outward expression the habits, mannerisms, dress, speech expressions, and behavior of the world out from which God saved him, thus not giving a true expression of what he is, a cleansed, regenerated child of God, but instead, hiding the Lord Jesus who should be seen in the life of the Christian. It is the believer masquerading in the costume of the world. The word "lusts" is literally "passionate desires," here, as the context indicates, evil desires. The word "lust," when the A.V. was translated, referred to any craving or strong desire, good or bad, as the context indicated. Today, its meaning is confined almost entirely to that of an immoral desire.

Verse fifteen

The word "as" is from *kata* which has the root idea of "down," thus "domination." Vincent suggests, "after the pattern of the One who called you." "Holy" is to be taken here as a noun, not an adjective. "The Holy One" was a title of God well established in His relation to Gentile Christians. "Be" is from *ginomai* which is not the verb of being, but of "becoming." It is ingressive aorist here, signifying entrance into a new state. Those who at one time were wholly controlled by their evil cravings, had through salva-

---

1. *Nuggets*, pp. 26-28.

tion entered into a new state of being, that of inward holiness, by virtue of the residence in them of the Holy Spirit, and now they were to see to it that that inward holiness found outward expression in their lives. The word "holy" in Greek means literally, "set apart." Thus, a holy person is one set apart from sin to righteousness. It has in it the idea of separation. Thus it is a separated life of which Peter is speaking. The word "saint" is the translation of the same word. Furthermore, they were not to cover up their characters as Christians by outwardly assuming a masquerade costume patterned after their former worldly garments. The second use of the word "holy" is in the plural. They were to become holy ones in their personal experience. "Conversation" is the translation of a Greek word meaning "behavior." Today the word "conversation" means "talk." In A.D. 1611, when the A.V. was translated, it meant "manner of life, behavior." One must be careful to take into account changes of meaning in the case of certain words in the English Bible.

Verse sixteen

The words "it is written" are the translation of a verb in the perfect tense in Greek, which tense speaks of a past completed action having present results. One could translate more fully, "It has been written and as a present result is on record." Peter was quoting from Leviticus 11:44 which was written by the stylus of Moses, the inspired man of God, 1500 B.C., and probably on clay tablets. At the time of the writing of this letter, A.D. 60, Peter spoke of Moses' words as still on record, the eternal, unchanging Word of God. Our Lord used the same expression in Matthew 4:4, 7, and Satan used it in 4:6 when quoting, rather misquoting, Psalm 91:11, 12. In the words "I am holy," the "I" is intensive, the emphatic use of the personal pronoun being in the Greek text. It is, "I, in contradistinction to anyone else, am holy."

FULLER TRANSLATION

(13) *Wherefore, having put out of the way, once for all, everything that would impede the free action of your mind, be calm and collected in spirit, and set your hope perfectly, wholly, and unchangeably, without doubt and despondency upon the grace that is being brought to you upon the occasion of the revelation of Jesus Christ; (14) as children of obedience not assuming an outward expression which would not be true of your inner life, an expression patterned after that which you formerly had in the ignorance of your passionate desires, (15) but after the pattern of the One who called you, the Holy One, also yourselves become holy persons in every kind of behavior, (16) because it has been written and as a present result is on record, Holy ones be ye, because I am holy.*

6.

THE INFINITE COST OF REDEMPTION (1:17-21)

Verse seventeen

THE "if" does not introduce an hypothesis but a fulfilled condition. "Since," or "in view of the fact," is the idea in the word. These to whom Peter was writing, were Christians. They were calling upon the Father. The idea in the Greek is, "in view of the fact that you call on as Father." That is, they recognized God as their Father since they had been brought into the family of God in salvation. They appealed to Him as a child would appeal to its father. What a blessed thought to give us encouragement in our praying, faith that the answer is sure, and a sweet feeling of nearness to God. To think that He is our Father and we are His children. To think that He regards us as His children, and thus the objects of His special care and love.

Peter describes Him as being One "who without respect of persons judgeth according to every man's work." The words "without respect of persons" are the translation of one word in Greek which means literally, "does not receive face." That is, God does not receive anybody's face. He is impartial. Outward appearance, wealth, culture, social position, family background, education, beauty, intellect, all things that more or less sway the opinions of man, do not count with God when it comes to appraising a person's character or worthiness. "The Lord seeth not as man seeth; for man looketh on the outward appearance, but the Lord looketh on the heart" (I Sam. 16:7). God, Peter says, judges each man's work with impartiality. And yet we are not to understand that He is a critical judge trying always to find a defect or flaw in our conduct or service. The Greek word is found oftener in a good than in a bad sense. That is, God's impartiality is an honest appraisal of things, while His heart is always with His child and goes out to him in a spirit of love. That is beautifully brought out in the use of a particular Greek word in I Corinthians 3:13, which verse and its context refer to the judgment of the believer's works at the Judgment Seat of Christ. There are two Greek words which mean "to put to the test," one meaning "to put to the test in order to discover what evil or good there may be in a person," the other, "to put to the test in order to sanction or approve the good one finds in that person."[1] The latter is used in our verse. God expects to find in the life of each saint that upon which He can put His approval, for the Holy Spirit produces good works in all the saints, more in those who are definitely subjected to His control.

In view of this impartial judgment of God, the Christian is exhorted to pass the time of his sojourning in fear. The word "pass" is the translation of a Greek word meaning "to conduct one's self, to order one's conduct or behavior." The word "sojourning" is from a word meaning literally "to have a home alongside of," and refers to a person living in a foreign land alongside of people who are not of his kind. Here it refers to children of God living far from their heavenly home, in foreign territory, on a planet that has a usurper, Satan, as reigning monarch, the people of which are his subjects. The Christian must always live in the consciousness of the fact that he is being watched by the unsaved, that his responsibility is to bear a clear, ringing, genuine testimony to His God and Saviour by the kind of life he lives. Peter says he is to do this in fear. This fear has been defined as follows: "This fear is self-distrust; it is tenderness of conscience; it is vigilance against temptation; it is the fear which inspiration opposes to highmindedness in the admonition,

---

1. *Treasures*, pp. 126-131.

'be not high-minded but fear.' It is taking heed lest we fall; it is a constant apprehension of the deceitfulness of the heart, and of the insidiousness and power of inward corruption. It is the caution and circumspection which timidly shrinks from whatever would offend and dishonor God and the Saviour" (Vincent, quoting Wardlaw On Proverbs).

Verse eighteen

The word "know" in the Greek text speaks of a self-evident, intuitive knowledge. The word "redeemed" means "to set free by the payment of a ransom." The words "silver" and "gold" are in a diminutive form, referring to little silver and gold coins which were used to buy slaves out of slavery. The word "vain" is the translation of a Greek word which has in it the idea of an ineffectual attempt to do something, an unsuccessful effort to attain something. It is found in the sentence from an early secular document, "He vainly relates." Thus, the vain conversation from which the Christian is liberated is his manner of life before he was saved which failed to meet the standards of God. It was a futile life, in that it did not measure up to that for which human life was created, to glorify God.

This manner of life they had received by tradition from their fathers. The phrase "received by tradition from your fathers" is the translation of one Greek word which means literally "given from father." That is, this futile manner of life was passed down to the son from the father through the channels of heredity, teaching, example, and environment. The child is born in sin, that is, comes into being with a totally depraved nature, and if the parents are unsaved, comes into a home where evil customs and practices are observed. What the child inherits, Peter calls a futile manner of life. From this futile manner of life the recipients of this letter were delivered.

Verse nineteen

The Greek word "precious" has a two-fold meaning, "costly" in the sense of value, and "highly esteemed or held in honor." The blood of Christ is costly, essentially and intrinsically precious because it is God's blood (Acts 20:28), for Deity became incarnate in humanity. For that reason it is highly honored by God the Father. The order of the words in the Greek text is beautiful. Please observe same in the fuller translation. It was not little silver and gold coins which set these Christians free from sin, but the blood of Christ.

Verse twenty

"Foreordained" in the Greek text means "to designate beforehand" to a position or function. In the councils of the triune God, the Lord Jesus was the Lamb marked out for sacrifice. "Foundation" is the translation of a word meaning literally "to throw down," and was used of the laying of the foundation of a house. It speaks of the act of the transcendent God throwing out into space the universe by speaking the word. "World" in the Greek text is *kosmos,* which speaks of an ordered system, and here of that perfect universe which left the hands of the Creator. The Greeks have a word for a rude, unformed mass, a word from which we get our English word "chaos." In Genesis 1:1 we have a *kosmos,* a system in which order prevails, and in 1:2, a *chaos,* a rude unformed mass, the latter the result of God's curse because of Lucifer's sin. Before this universe was created, the Lord Jesus had been foreordained to be the Saviour of lost sinners, and the saints had been foreordained to become recipients of the salvation He would procure for lost sinners at the Cross (Eph. 1:4; Rom. 8:29).[1]

The word "manifest" in the Greek means "to make or become visible." It was the invisible God who in the Person

---

1. *Bypaths,* pp. 99-105.

of His Son was made visible to human eyesight by assuming a human body and human limitations.

Verse twenty-one

The words in the Greek text translated "do believe" refer to the identity of the recipients, speaking of the fact that they were believers, rather than of the act of believing. "From" is the translation of a preposition meaning "out from." "Dead" refers not to the state of death, but to individuals who are dead. It is a plural noun in the Greek. Our Lord was raised out from among those who were dead. They stayed in that condition called death, whereas He was given life. This belief in God of which Peter speaks is not a mental acceptance of the fact of His existence, but a heart faith in the God who saves sinners in answer to their faith in the resurrected Lord Jesus who died for them.

FULLER TRANSLATION

(17) *And in view of the fact that you call on as Father Him who judges, not with a partiality based upon mere outward appearance, but with impartiality in accordance with each individual's work, in fear order your behavior during the time of your residence as a foreigner, (18) knowing as you do, that not by means of corruptible things, little coins of silver and gold, were you set free once for all by the payment of ransom money, out of and away from your futile manner of life handed down from generation to generation, (19) but with costly blood highly honored, blood as of a lamb that is without blemish and spotless, the blood of Christ, (20) who indeed was foreordained before the foundation of the universe was laid, but was visibly manifested at the closing years of the times for your sake, (21) who through Him are believers in God, the One who raised Him out from among those who are dead and gave Him glory, so that your faith and hope might be in God.*

7.

THE LOVE FOR THE BRETHREN (1:22-25)

Verses twenty-two — twenty-five

THE recipients of this letter had purified their souls with the result that they came to love their Christian brethren with an unfeigned love, the implication being clear that at one time these Christians were guilty of feigning love for certain of their brothers in Christ. The word "unfeigned" is the translation of the Greek word from which we get our word "hypocrite," with the letter Alpha prefixed which makes it mean "not a hypocrite." The Greek word for "hypocrite" was used of an actor on the Greek stage, one who played the part of another. The word means literally, "to judge under," and was used of someone giving off his judgment from behind a screen or mask. Some of these to whom Peter was writing, had put a mask of feigned love over their usual countenances when associating with certain others of their brethren.

There were two conditions in the early Church which were responsible for this hypocrisy. Some Christians were tempted to go back to their old associates, preferring their company to that of their Christian brethren. This is intimated in 4:3, where the apostle suggests that they had plenty of time before salvation to run in sin with the world. Those Christians who went back to their former worldly associates and preferred their company to that of believers, would naturally assume an attitude of love towards the latter. Then there was that other condition in which different grades of society were represented in the early Church, slaves and freeman, rich and poor, educated and illiterate. The privileged were slow to take the under-privileged to themselves in a Christian brotherly way. This is hinted at in 2:1 in the words "hypocrisies" and "evil speakings," the latter expression referring to the act of deprecating another, literally "speaking a person down."

The particular word for love used here is *phile,* a love called out of one's heart by the pleasure one takes in the person loved. It is a love of "liking." One likes another person because that person is like himself in the sense that that person reflects in his own personality the same characteristics, the same likes and dislikes that he himself has. It is an affection or fondness, a purely human attachment for another, and perfectly legitimate. This particular Greek word for love was used advisedly by the inspired apostle. The context in which it is found is concerned with one's attitude toward one's fellow Christian as contrasted to one's former worldly associates. This attitude with respect to the latter should be necessarily changed at the time of salvation. The necessity for the change is based upon a change in the person's character from that of a sinner to that of a saint. The saying goes, "Birds of a feather flock together." The species has an attachment for itself based upon similarity of character. Thus an affection or fondness for another based upon the likeness of that other to one's self is in the mind of Peter here.

Now, the thing that caused some of these Christians to revert to their former worldly associates was failure to obey the Word of God. Consequently, their heart-life became sinful. Therefore, they preferred their former sinful companions to their fellow Christians. But when they started to obey the Word again, their souls were purified, and they came to have that fondness and affection for their Christian brethren which is the normal condition among saints who are living lives of obedience to God's Word. The love which they showed toward other believers was an unassumed one. It came from the heart. Then again, obedience to the Word would cause the upper classes of society to have a fondness

and affection for the lower classes, in tha
off all classes and distinctions in the spiri
stitutes the saints an aristocracy of hea
seen on an infinitely high plane, in Christ

The words "have purified" are from a pe
the Greek. That is, a past completed proc
sistent, habitual obedience to the Word, h̲a̲u̲ ̲r̲e̲sulted in the
purifying of their souls as they obeyed, with the result that
their souls were in a present state of purification. They also
rectified an existing evil practice in their lives, that of a
hypocritical affection for their Christian brethren. The les-
son for us is that when we obey God's Word, our heart-life
is being purified, and this purification puts sin out of our
experience.

To those who were now loving their brethren in the sense
of a fondness and affection for them, God gives the exhortation, "See that ye love one another with a pure heart fervently." The question arises, "Why does God exhort those
to love one another who are already loving one another?"
The answer is found in the use of another distinctive word
for "love," *agape*, which Peter uses. This word speaks of a
love which in its classical usage refers to a love called out of
one's heart by the preciousness of the person loved, which
usage is carried over into the New Testament, but which word
has an additional content of meaning poured into it by the
way it is used in certain contexts such as John 3:16, where
the idea of self-sacrifice for the benefit of the person loved is
added to its classical meaning, I Corinthians 13, where
the constituent elements of its Biblical usage are listed, and
I John 4:8, where it is said to refer to the love that God is.
Thus, the exhortation is to love one's brother Christian because he is precious to God, and to love him with a love that
is willing to sacrifice one's self for the benefit of that brother,
a love that causes one to be long suffering toward him, a love
that makes one treat him kindly, a love that so causes one
to rejoice in the welfare of another that there is no room for

in the heart, a love that is not jealous, a love that keeps
e from boasting of one's self, a love that keeps one from
bearing one's self in a lofty manner, a love that keeps one
from acting unbecomingly, a love that keeps one from seeking one's own rights, a love that keeps one from becoming
angry, a love that does not impute evil, a love that does not
rejoice in iniquity but in the truth, a love that bears up
against all things, believes all things, hopes all things, endures
all things. That is the kind of love which God says one
Christian should have for another. These Christians to whom
Peter was writing already had a fondness and an affection
for one another. The feeling of fondness and affection was
perfectly proper in itself, but it could degenerate into an
attachment for another which would be very selfish. But if
these Christians would blend the two kinds of love, saturate
the human fondness and affection with the divine love with
which they are exhorted to love one another, then that
human affection would be transformed and elevated to a
heavenly thing. Then the fellowship of saint with saint would
be a heavenly fellowship, glorifying to the Lord Jesus, and
most blessed in its results to themselves. There is plenty of
the *phile*[1] fondness and affection among the saints, and too
little of the *agape*[1] divine love.

But how to have such a heavenly love for one another,
that is the problem, one may say. The answer is simple. This
love is produced in the heart of the saint who is definitely
subjected to the control of the Holy Spirit. This love is one
of His fruits (Gal. 5:22). Thus God exhorts the saints to
love one another with a divine love, and then produces that
love in their hearts as they trust Him to do that for them and
by the action of their free will choose to be loving and exert
themselves to act in a loving way towards their brethren.[2]
The best Greek texts do not have the words "through the
Spirit." It is true that we can only obey the Word as the
Holy Spirit gives us the desire and the power to do so, and

---

1. *Bypaths*, pp. 109-123.
2. *Riches*, pp. 74-114.

these are given to us as we yield to Him. But we have left
these words out of the fuller translation since they do not
appear in the best Greek texts. The word "another" is a
reciprocal pronoun in Greek and thus refers here to a reciprocal love. The words "with a pure heart," are literally,
"out of a pure heart." The word "fervently" is the translation of a Greek word meaning "an intense strain." Verses
23-25 are sufficiently clear in the A.V., the Greek words involved do not need any special treatment, and the fuller
translation offered will bring out any added shades of meaning which are in the Greek text. Therefore, there is no
special exegesis offered of these verses.

FULLER TRANSLATION

(22) *Wherefore, having purified your souls by means of
your obedience to the truth, resulting in not an assumed but
a genuine affection and fondness for the brethren, an affection and fondness that springs from your hearts by reason of
the pleasure you take in them; from the heart love each other
with an intense reciprocal love that springs from your hearts
because of your estimation of the preciousness of the brethren,
and which is divinely self-sacrificial in its essence,* (23) *having
been begotten again through the Word of God which lives
and abides;* (24) *for every kind of flesh is as grass, and its
every kind of glory is as the flower of grass. The grass withers
away, and the flower falls off,* (25) *but the Word of the Lord
abides forever. And this is the Word which in the declaration
of the good news was preached to you.*

8.

THE BELIEVER-PRIEST'S SPIRITUAL FOOD (2:1-5)

Verse one

"WHEREFORE" goes back to the fact of the new life imparted (1:23), and argues in 2:1-3 that therefore a new kind of experience is demanded of the believer. "Laying aside" is from a participle that has imperative force. In view of the fact that divine life has been imparted to the believer, it is imperative that he "put away once for all" any sins that may be in his life. The preposition prefixed to the verb implies separation. The believer is commanded to separate himself from sin. This act of separating himself from sin must be a once for all action, as the tense of the participle suggests. There must be a complete right-about face.

Peter then singles out five sins that the recipients of this letter were guilty of. The Greek word translated "malice" refers to any kind of wickedness. "Guile" is the translation of a word which in its verb form means "to catch with bait," and in the noun which Peter uses means "craftiness." The word "hypocrisies" is the transliteration of the Greek word *hupokriseis* which means literally "to judge under," as a person giving off his judgment from behind a screen or mask. The true identity of the person is covered up. It refers to acts of impersonation or deception. It was used of an actor on the Greek stage. Taken over into the New Testament, it referred to a person we call a hypocrite, one who assumes the mannerisms, speech, and character of someone else, thus hiding his true identity. Christianity requires that believers should be open and above-board. They should be them-

selves. Their lives should be like an open book, easily read.
The word "evil speakings" are in the Greek text "speaking
down" a person, referring to the act of defaming, slandering,
speaking against another.

Verse two

"Newborn babes" is from the Greek word *brephos,* used
only here in the New Testament in its metaphorical sense.
Luke uses it (2:16) of the babe in the manger. In classical
Greek it was used of a babe at the breast. Peter probably
took the figure from Isaiah 28:9, "Whom will he teach knowledge? Them that are weaned from the milk and drawn from
the breasts." The recipients of this letter are called just-born
infants, speaking of the recency of the Christian life in their
case. The Greek word translated "desire" speaks of an intense yearning. That which they are exhorted to have is an
intense yearning for milk. The word "sincere" is from the
same Greek word translated in 2:1, "deceit," but with the
Greek letter Alpha prefixed which makes the word mean the
opposite to what it meant before. It is guileless milk, thus
unadulterated. It has nothing added to it. The Word of
God has no ulterior motives like so many human teachings,
but has for its only purpose that of nourishing the soul. The
words "of the word" are from an article and adjective in the
Greek text speaking of the quality of this milk, literally,
rational as opposed to ceremonial, thus spiritual. The word
"milk" here does not refer to that part of the Word of God
which is in contrast to the meat or solid food of the Word
as in Hebrews 5:13, 14, but to the Word of God in general.
The words "that ye may grow thereby" could also be rendered "in order that ye might be nourished up." There is a
phrase in the Greek text not brought out in the translation,
"resulting in your making progress in your salvation."

The prerequisite to the act of intensely yearning for the
Word of God is the act of once for all putting sin out of our

lives. Sin in the life destroys the appetite for the Word. The Christian who tries to find satisfaction in the husks of the world, has no appetite left for the things of God. His heart is filled with the former and has no room for the latter. A healthy infant is a hungry infant. A spiritually healthy Christian is a hungry Christian. This solves the problem of why so many children of God have so little love for the Word.

Verse three

The "if" is a fulfilled condition. They as newborn babes had tasted the Word of God, and had found in it that the Lord was gracious. The word "gracious" is the translation of a Greek word used in Luke 5:39 where it is translated "better." The word means literally, "excellent."

Verse four

The words "to whom coming" in the Greek text do not refer to the initial act of the sinner coming to the Lord Jesus for salvation, but indicate a close and habitual approach and an intimate association made by faith when the believer realizes the presence of and seeks communion and fellowship with his Lord. The words "as unto" are in italics in the translation, showing that they are not in the Greek text, and were supplied by the translators to help give the sense of the passage. But here we have no metaphor. There is no such thing in existence as a living stone. God is that Living Stone to whom we come. The article is not used with the expression, showing that emphasis is placed upon character or quality. He is in character a Living Stone.

The word "disallowed" is the translation of a word that refers to the act of putting someone or something to the test for the purpose of putting one's approval upon that person and thus receiving him, this act of testing being carried to the point where no further testing is needed, with the result that one comes to the settled conclusion that the one tested does not meet the requirements of the test and is therefore disapproved, repudiated. This Living Stone in the Person of God the Son became incarnate, lived for thirty-three years in the midst of Israel, offered Himself as its Messiah, was examined by official Israel for the purpose of approving Him as its Messiah, and then repudiated because He was not what official Israel wanted in a Messiah. What a commentary on the totally depraved condition of man's heart.

The word "chosen" is not a verb in the Greek text but a noun, literally "a chosen-out one," thus "elect." "Precious" is the translation of a Greek word used in Luke 7:2, describing the centurion's servant as "dear" to him. The word speaks of one being held in honor and as dear to another. "Of God" is literally "in the sight of God."

Verse five

Believers are lively or living stones (the same Greek word is used for both Christ and the believer) because their life is Christ. This spiritual house is not the local church nor even a group of saints, but the Mystical Body of Christ, the Church Universal, for Peter is addressing believers in five Roman provinces. The words "holy priesthood" in the Greek text are preceded by a preposition showing purpose. Thus we translate, "to be a holy priesthood." The words "to offer up" are the translation of a word used in the Greek translation of the Old Testament of the act of the priest bearing the sacrifice up to the brazen altar. The latter was four and one-half feet high and was approached by an incline up which the priest carried the sacrifice. The word itself means literally, "to carry up." Thus the Church is an unlimited priesthood to offer upon the altar of the consecrated, dedicated heart of the believer, spiritual sacrifices, not animal sacrifices as in the case of the Levitical priests, but the activities of the human spirit of man energized by the Holy Spirit. The word "acceptable" in the Greek text means literally "to receive to one's self with pleasure." What a blessing it is to think that God is pleased with the spirituality He finds in the life of a Christian. He was pleased with the sacrifices offered up in Old Testament times in that they spoke of the Lord Jesus. He is pleased with the spiritual sacrifices of the believer because He sees in them a reflection of the Lord Jesus.

FULLER TRANSLATION

(1) *Wherefore, putting away once for all, all wickedness, and all craftiness, and hypocrisies, and envies, and all slanderings, (2) as newborn infants, intensely yearn for the unadulterated spiritual milk in order that you may be nourished and make progress in (your) salvation, (3) in view of the fact that you have tasted that the Lord is excellent; (4) toward whom we are constantly drawing near, Himself in character a Living Stone, indeed by men repudiated after they had tested Him for the purpose of approving Him, in which investigation they found Him to be that which did not meet their specifications, but in the sight of God a chosen-out One and held in honor; (5) you yourselves also as living stones are being built up a spiritual house, to be a priesthood that is holy, bringing up to God's altars spiritual sacrifices which are received by God through the mediatorship of Jesus Christ.*

9.

THE CHIEF CORNERSTONE (2:6-10)

Verse six

THIS Living Stone, the Lord Jesus, becomes the Chief
Cornerstone of the temple, the Church, the One who is
not only its foundation (Matt. 16:16, 18),[1] but also that
which holds the Church together. The word "elect" is literally "a chosen-out one." The word "precious" has the idea
of "held in honor." The word "confounded" is the translation of a Greek word that means "to be put to shame" in
the sense of being defeated or deceived in some hope.

Verse seven

The words "he is" are supplied by the translators in an
effort to make the meaning of the Greek plain to the English
reader. They are not in the Greek text. *Expositor's Greek
Testament* offers the following: "The 'precious'-ness of the
stone is for you who believe but for the unbelievers it is . . .
'a stone of stumbling'." Evidently Peter is showing the contrast between what the Living Stone means to believers and
what He becomes to the unbelievers because they refuse to
allow Him to become precious to them. One could translate,
"To you therefore who are believers, the Living Stone is
precious." The words "Living Stone" are taken from verse 4
where they appear in the Greek text. The word "disobedient"
is the translation of a word literally meaning "disbelieving."
"Disallowed" has the same meaning as in verse 4, which
please see. The Living Stone which is precious to believers
and a stone of stumbling and a rock of offense to unbelievers,

---

1. *Nuggets*, pp. 55-57.

God has chosen for the head cornerstone. It was the builders of Israel, the spiritual leaders of the nation, that repudiated the Living Stone after investigating Him, and yet God in His grace made Him a Head Cornerstone to these latter, if they would accept Him as such. The door of mercy was not closed to them.

Verse eight

The words "a stone of stumbling" are the translation of *lithos,* "a loose stone in the path," and *proskommatos* meaning "to cut against," which altogether mean "an obstacle against which one strikes." The words "rock of offence" are from *petra,* "a ledge rising out of the ground," and *skandalou,* "a trap set to trip one." Our word "scandal" comes from the latter word. These who are disobedient (the literal Greek has it "non-persuasable") are appointed to stumble at the Word, which is the penalty for refusal to believe it. "By faith we understand" (Heb. 11:3), is the God-ordained way. Thus, unbelievers find the Living Stone, which is precious to believers, an obstacle against which they strike, and a scandal, that which offends them.

Verse nine

The "ye" is emphatic in the Greek text. Literally, "but as for you," in contrast to the disobedient of verse 8. "Generation" is from a Greek word meaning "a race, a body with a common life and descent." It does not mean here a group of individuals living within the span of a lifetime. The word "royal" is the translation of the Greek word for "king." The Levitical priesthood were only priests. Believers in this dispensation are king-priests, associated with the Lord Jesus who is a priest after the order of Melchisedec, a king-priest. The word "nation" is the translation of a Greek word meaning "a multitude of people of the same nature." The word "holy" in the Greek text means literally "set apart for the service of Deity." The word "peculiar" here is used in a way not often seen today. The Greek word means literally "to

make around," that is, to make something and then to sur-
round it with a circle, thus indicating ownership. The same
verb is used in the Septuagint translation of Isaiah 43:21
which reads, "This people have I formed for myself." The
word "peculiar" today usually means "odd, strange." But it
is not so used here. The Greek word speaks of the unique,
private, personal ownership of the saints by God. Each saint
is God's unique possession just as if that saint were the only
human being in existence. The words "show forth" in the
Greek text refer to a spoken message. The word "praises" is
not the translation of the Greek word customarily used to
indicate praise, but of one which means "excellencies, gracious dealings, glorious attributes." The word "into" refers
here not merely to locality, but to a result, that of the saints
being participants of the light that God is in His nature. We
are made creatures of light.

FULLER TRANSLATION

(6) *Because of this, it is contained in Scripture, Behold, I
lay in Zion a Stone, one chosen out, a cornerstone, held in
honor, and the one who rests his faith on Him shall not be
defeated.* (7) *To you therefore who are believers, the Living
Stone is precious; but to those who are disbelievers, the Stone
which the builders repudiated after they had tested Him for
the purpose of approving Him, finding Him to be that which
did not meet their specifications, this Stone became a Head
Corner Stone,* (8) *and an obstacle stone against which one cuts,
and a rock which trips one, even to those who because they are
non-persuasable, stumble up against the Word, to which
(action of stumbling) they were indeed appointed.* (9) *But
as for you, you are a race chosen out, king-priests, a set-apart
nation, a people formed for God's own possession, in order
that you might proclaim abroad the excellencies of the One
who out of darkness called you into participation in His
marvelous light,* (10) *who at one time were not a people,
but now are the people of God; who were not subjects of
mercy, but now have become objects of mercy.*

10.

THE DEPORTMENT OF THE CHRISTIAN AMONGST
THE UNSAVED (2:11-17)

Verse eleven

THE words "dearly beloved" are the translation of one word in Greek, plural in number, the distinctive word used of God's divine love. This is not the "dearly beloved" of the pastor addressing his congregation on the Lord's Day morning, but Peter reminding them that they are dearly loved-ones of God. The Greek word "beseech" is literally, "I exhort, urge, I beg of you, please." While it is Peter writing, yet it is the great God of the universe saying to His blood-bought children, "I beg of you, please." Think of the love and humility, the infinite condescension of God that stoops to address a creature of His handiwork whom He could command.

The word "stranger" is the translation of a Greek word meaning "to have one's home alongside of," thus a "sojourner." "Pilgrims" is from a word which literally means "to settle down alongside of pagans." The two words describe the Christian in his position in this world. He has made his home alongside of the unsaved and settled down amongst them, a sojourner and one that is a stranger to them in that he is different from them. The exhortation to abstain from fleshly lusts is based upon the fact that Christians are living in the midst of the unsaved. They have a testimony to maintain and a message to give. The word "abstain" is literally, "hold yourself constantly back from" fleshly lusts, the implication being clear that the fallen nature whose power over the believer was broken when he was saved is still there with its sin-ward pull. We are told to hold ourselves back from doing the things which before salvation wrought its work in our beings we did naturally. The word "lusts" is literally "cravings, strong desires," good or bad, depending upon the context, here evil cravings coming from the totally depraved nature.

The word "which" has a qualitative aspect in the original, "which are of such a nature as to." "War" is from a verb which speaks of the act of carrying on a military campaign. The word "against" is the translation of a Greek word whose root meaning is "down."

Verse twelve

"Having" has a durative aspect in the Greek. It is a steady holding of our conversation up to a certain standard. "Conversation" is the translation of a Greek word speaking of one's manner of life. The word meant that when the A.V. was translated. Today, the meaning of the word is limited to the act of speaking. We must be careful to note the obsolete words in the A.V., and not interpret them in their present day meaning. The word "honest" is the translation of a Greek word that speaks of goodness which is beautiful, an outer goodness that strikes the eye. Alford translates it "comely"; Robertson, "seemly." Our manner of life is honest when our lives are in accordance with what we are inwardly, cleansed, regenerated children of God. We give others an honest testimony and picture of what we really are inwardly. "Seemly" also speaks of the necessity of maintaining an outward testimony that is in conformity with our profession. The word "Gentiles" is from the Greek word referring here, not to Gentiles as in contrast to Jews, but to the unsaved world, the world of people without Christ.

The word "whereas" is literally "in what thing," that is, in the very thing in which the world speaks evil of a Christian,

namely, of his Christian life, which latter makes it necessary
for him to diverge from the things of the world and live a life
of separation. The words "speak against" are literally "speak
down," referring to the act of adversely criticizing a person.
The separated life of a Christian is one of the most powerful
means God has of convicting the world of its sin. The world
does not like its sin uncovered, hence the persecution which
it directs against the separated Christian. How the people of
the world watch the Christian. The word "behold" in the
Greek text means "to view carefully as a personal witness."

The word "visitation" is the translation of the Greek word
which is also rendered "bishop, overseer." It means "to observe, inspect, oversee" in its verb form, and "one who over-
sees or observes," in its noun form which is used here. The
day of visitation is "the day of looking upon." Wherever this
word is used in the New Testament and translated "visit" or
"visitation," it refers to the visitation of God's mercy and
grace.[1] Here it refers to the day when as Vincent puts it,
"God shall look upon these wanderers as a pastor over his
flock, and shall become the overlooker or bishop of their souls."
The same Greek word is translated "Bishop" in 2:25. The
good works of Christians, their beautiful and separated lives,
are used of God as one of the means of bringing lost sinners
to the Lord Jesus. When they are saved, God becomes the
spiritual overseer of their souls. Then these sinners saved by
grace will glorify Him because of the Christlike lives of certain Christians that caused them to want the Saviour too.

Verse thirteen

The words "submit yourselves" are the translation of a
Greek military term meaning "to arrange in military fashion
under the command of a leader." One could translate, "put
yourselves in the attitude of submission to." The exhortation
is not merely to obey ordinances, but to create and maintain

1. *Treasures*, pp. 61-64.

that attitude of heart which will always lead one to obey them. "Ordinances of man" refer to human institutions, such as the laws of the land. Christians are to do this because of their testimony to the Lord Jesus.

Verse fifteen

There are no Greek word studies in verse 14. The words "put to silence" are the translation of a Greek word which means "to close the mouth with a muzzle." It was used of the muzzling of an ox (I Cor. 9:9). It means here, "to reduce to silence." Matthew uses it (22:34) of our Lord putting the Sadducees to silence, and Mark, of stilling the storm on the Sea of Galilee (4:39). The word "ignorance" in the Greek text speaks of want of knowledge, not in the sense of want of acquaintance, but want of understanding. The word "foolish" is the translation of a Greek word speaking of lack of reason, reflection, and intelligence.

FULLER TRANSLATION

(11) *Divinely loved ones, I beg of you, please, as those who are sojourning alongside of a foreign population (should), be constantly holding yourselves back from the fleshly cravings, cravings of such a nature that, like an army carrying on a military campaign, they are waging war, hurling themselves down upon your soul; (12) holding your manner of life among the unsaved steadily beautiful in its goodness, in order that in the thing in which they defame you as those who do evil (namely, in your Christianity), because of your works beautiful in their goodness which they are constantly, carefully, and attentively watching, they may glorify God in the day of His overseeing care. (13) Put yourselves in the attitude of submission to, thus giving yourselves to the obedience of, every human regulation for the sake of the Lord, whether to the king as one who is supereminent, (14) or to governors as*

those sent by him to inflict vengeance upon those who do evil, and to give praise to those who do good; (15) for so is the will of God, that by doing good you might be reducing to silence the ignorance of men who are unreflecting and unintelligent; (16) doing all this as those who have their liberty, and not as those who are holding their liberty as a cloak of wickedness, but as those who are God's bondmen. (17) Pay honor to all, be loving the brotherhood, be fearing God, be paying honor to the king.

11.

A PORTRAIT OF THE SUFFERING SERVANT OF JEHOVAH (2:18-25)

Verse eighteen

THE particular Greek word translated "servants" indicates that these were household slaves. They were Christian slaves serving for the most part in the homes of pagan masters. The fact that Peter singles them out for special admonitions indicates that slaves, as a class, formed a large part of the early Christian community. The slaves are exhorted to put themselves in subjection to their absolute lords and masters. They are to do this to the good and gentle ones. Some of these pagan masters had what the poet calls "the milk of human kindness." They were good to their slaves. The Greek word translated "good," refers to inner intrinsic goodness. They were good at heart. The word "gentle" in the Greek refers to that disposition which is mild, yielding, indulgent. It is derived from a Greek word meaning, "not being unduly rigorous." Alford translates, "where not strictness of legal right, but consideration for another is the rule of practice." The one word "reasonable" sums up its meaning pretty well.

The slaves were to put themselves into subjection as well to the froward. The Greek word means "unfair, surly, froward." The word "froward" is from the Anglo-Saxon word "from-ward," namely, "averse." The masters had their faces dead set against these Christian slaves. We can understand that attitude when we remember that these slaves lived lives of singular purity, meekness, honesty, willingness to serve, and

obedience in the households of their heathen masters. This
was a powerful testimony for the gospel, and brought them
under conviction of sin. All this irritated them, and they re-
acted in a most unpleasant way toward their slaves, whom
they would punish without provocation. Yet they did not
want to sell these Christian slaves and buy pagan ones, for
the Christian slaves served them better. So they just had to
make the best of the situation.

Verse nineteen

The word "this" is neuter in the Greek text, literally "this
thing," namely, obedience to masters who are averse to their
slaves, and patience under unjust punishment meted out by
these masters. "Thankworthy" is the translation of a Greek
word referring to an action that is beyond the ordinary course
of what might be expected, and is therefore commendable.
The unsaved slave would react toward unjust punishment in
a surly, rebellious, sullen, vindictive manner. That would be
the expected and ordinary thing. But Peter exhorts these
Christian slaves to be obedient to these unjust and cruel masters, and when punished unjustly to behave in a meek, patient, and forgiving manner. This would be an action beyond
the ordinary course of what might be expected, and would
therefore be commendable. The motive for acting thus, Peter
tells them, is "for conscience toward God." The idea here is
not that of conscientiousness in the ordinary sense, but of the
Christian slave's conscious sense of his relation to God. He
has a testimony to maintain before his pagan master. He has
the Lord Jesus Christ to emulate and reflect in his life.

The Greek word translated "thankworthy," referring to an
action which is beyond the ordinary course of what might be
expected and is therefore commendable, is the word used in
the New Testament when it speaks of God's grace. When used
in the latter connection, it refers to God's action of stepping
down from His judgment throne and in infinite love taking

upon Himself the guilt and penalty of human sin in order that He might satisfy the just requirements of His law which we disobeyed, thus making possible the righteous bestowal of His mercy on the basis of justice satisfied. It is a favor done out of the pure generosity of God's heart for beings who not only did not deserve salvation but deserved divine wrath. This act of God at the Cross is surely beyond the ordinary course of what might be expected, and is therefore commendable. This is just another proof of the divine source of the Bible. Such an act of grace never occurred to sinful man because it is beyond the ordinary course of action which would be expected of a member of the human race. The race simply does not act that way.

Verse twenty

The word "glory" is not the translation of the word *doxa* which is used when the glory of God is spoken of, but of *kleos,* found only here in the New Testament, and which means "fame, praise, glory, good report." The word "buffeted" in the Greek text speaks of the act of striking with the fist. It is in the present tense which usually refers to progressive action. The word here could be translated "pummeled." These Christian slaves were being pummeled by their irate masters, the only offence of the former being that they lived Christlike lives which were used of the Holy Spirit to convict the latter of sin.

The same Greek word is used in Matthew 26:67 where the Lord Jesus was pummeled by the frenzied Jewish mob. Isaiah 52:14 gives us a picture of our Lord after the pummeling which He received at the hands of the Jews; "As many were astonied at thee; his visage was so marred more than any man, and his form more than the sons of men." The literal rendering of this verse according to Hebrew scholars is as follows, "So marred from the form of man was His aspect that His appearance was not that of a son of man," namely, not human.

This passage bears the marks of Peter's memories of that awful night. His exhortation to these Christian slaves is that when they are being unjustly pummeled by their masters, they should remember the Lord Jesus and how He was unjustly pummeled, and for them, and react towards their masters as Jesus did to those who mistreated Him. They are to take this punishment patiently, and this would be acceptable with God. The word "acceptable" is the translation of the same Greek word rendered "thankworthy" in verse 19. Patient endurance of unjust punishment on the part of these slaves is in the sight of God an action that is beyond the ordinary course of what might be expected, and is therefore commendable.

Verse twenty-one

"Hereunto" is literally "into this" namely, the endurance of wrongful sufferings. The divine call of God to a lost sinner is an effectual call into salvation, and an accompaniment of that salvation is suffering for righteousness' sake, the natural result of the Christian's contact with the people of the world and their reaction towards the Lord Jesus who is seen in the life of the saint. Paul speaks of the same thing when he says, "For unto you it is given in the behalf of Christ, not only to believe on him, but also to suffer for his sake" (Phil. 1:29).

Then Peter reminds these slaves that Christ also suffered unjustly, for He the Just One, died on behalf of unjust ones. He suffered vicariously, that is, He paid the penalty of sin for lost sinners. Thus He suffered for these Christian slaves. They are suffering for Jesus in the sense that by their patient endurance of unjust punishment, they are bearing a powerful testimony to His saving grace. Peter's use of the word "also" puts the sufferings of these slaves on a new plane. They find comfort in knowing that someone else, and that person the Lord Jesus Himself, went through a like experience, that of suffering unjustly.

The word "leaving" is literally "leaving behind." When Peter used the Greek word here translated "example," he went back to his boyhood days for an illustration. The word means literally "writing under." It was used of words given children to copy, both as a writing exercise and as a means of impressing a moral. Sometimes it was used with reference to the act of tracing over written letters. Peter changes over easily from the idea of a child tracing over the writing of the writing-master to a Christian planting his feet in the foot-prints left by our Lord. In this context, these footprints are footprints of suffering. But the illustration holds good for our Lord's entire life. Just as a child slowly, with painstaking effort and close application, follows the shape of the letters of his teacher and thus learns to write, so saints should with like painstaking effort and by close application, endeavor to be like the Lord Jesus in their own personal lives. Or, as a small child endeavors to walk in the footprints made by his father's feet in the snow, so we are to follow in the path which our Lord took. The Greek word "follow" means literally "to take the same road" as someone else takes. We should walk the same road that Jesus walked, in short, be Christlike.

Verse twenty-two

The word "did" in the Greek text speaks of the fact of sin. Alford translates, "Who never in a single instance committed sin." The Greek word for "guile" is the same one found in 2:1, which verse please consult for full treatment of the word. The word speaks of craftiness or trickery. "Found" is the translation of a Greek word which, together with the negative with which it is used, speaks of a failure to find something after careful scrutiny.

Verse twenty-three

The Greek word translated "revile," Calvin defines as follows, "It is a harsher railing, which not only rebukes a man but also sharply bites him, and stamps him with open con-

tumely. It is to wound a man with an accursed sting." Thus
was the tender heart of the Lord Jesus wounded by totally depraved human nature. The words "suffered" and "threatened" have a progressive force in the original. Even continuous suffering at the hands of the mob did not elicit from our
Lord any retaliatory words. The word "but" in the Greek
text does not adversely contrast the two actions here, but re-
moves the thing previously negatived altogether out of our
field of view and substitutes something totally different. The
word "committed" is the translation of a Greek word which
means literally "to hand over." It means "to deliver something
to someone to keep, use, take care of, manage." Our Lord
kept on delivering over to God the Father both the revilers
and their revilings as both kept on wounding His loving heart.
It is for us to do the same thing when men revile us because
of our Christian testimony.

Verse twenty-four

The word "bare" is the translation of a word used in the
LXX, of the priest carrying the sacrifice up to the altar. The
brazen altar was four and one-half feet high, and was approached by an incline up which the priest bore the sacrifice. Alford says that this word belongs to the idea of sacrifice and is not to be disassociated from it. The Greek word
translated "tree" does not refer to a literal tree but to an object fashioned out of wood, in this case, the Cross. Thus, our
Lord, Himself the High Priest and the Sacrifice, carried our
sins as a burden of guilt up to the Cross.

The phrase "being dead to sins" is literally, "having become
off with respect to sins." It speaks of the action of God in
breaking the power of the sinful nature in the sinner when
he puts his faith in the Lord Jesus as Saviour. Henceforth
he need not be a slave to sin.

The word "stripes" in the Greek presents a picture of our
Lord's lacerated back after the scourging He endured at the

hands of the Roman soldier. The Romans used a scourge of cords or thongs to which latter were attached pieces of lead or brass, or small, sharp-pointed bones. Criminals condemned to crucifixion were ordinarily scourged before being executed. The victim was stripped to the waist and bound in a stooping position, with the hands behind the back, to a post or pillar. The suffering under the lash was intense. The body was frightfully lacerated. The Christian martyrs at Smyrna about A.D. 155 were so torn by the scourges that their veins were laid bare, and the inner muscles and sinews and even the bowels were exposed. The Greek word translated "stripes" refers to a bloody wale trickling with blood that arises under a blow. The word is singular, not plural. Peter remembered the body of our Lord after the scourging, the flesh so dreadfully mangled that the disfigured form appeared in his eyes as one single bruise.

Thus we have the portrait of the suffering Servant of Jehovah, His blessed face so pummeled by the hard fists of the mob that it did not look like a human face anymore, His back lacerated by the Roman scourge so that it was one mass of open, raw, quivering flesh trickling with blood, His heart torn with anguish because of the bitter, caustic, malevolent words hurled at Him. On that bleeding, lacerated back was laid the Cross. Unsaved reader, this was all for you, just as if you were the only lost person in the universe. The Lord Jesus died for you, in your stead, took your place on the Cross, paid your penalty, so that God could offer a salvation from sin based upon a justice satisfied. Will you not right now appropriate the Lord Jesus as your own personal Saviour, trust Him to save you? And saint, does not all this make you love the Lord Jesus more, soften and make more tender your heart? Does not all this make you say, "I can see the blood drops, red 'neath His thorny crown, from the cruel nail-wounds, now they are falling down; Lord, when I would wander from thy love away, let me see those blooddrops shed for

me that day?" The blood of Christ heals our sin in that He
by one offering put away sin forever. There is no room here
for the healing of illness through the blood of Jesus. The
Cross was a purely judicial matter. One goes to a hospital
when one is ill, and to a law court to take care of legal matters. In the great law court of the universe, the Judge offers
mercy on the basis of justice satisfied at the Cross. The matter of bodily illness is not mentioned in the context. Furthermore, the Greek word used here is not confined in its meaning
to physical healing. In Luke 4:18 it refers to the alleviation
of heartaches, and in Hebrews 12:13, to the rectifying of one's
conduct. In Matthew 13:15, it means, "to bring about (one's)
salvation." This passage cannot therefore be made to teach
the erroneous doctrine that healing of the body is to be found
in the atonement as salvation from sin is found at the Cross.
The context in which the word is found clearly decides the
meaning of the word here, not that of the healing of the body,
but that of the salvation of the soul.

Verse twenty-five

The word "Bishop" is the translation of the same Greek
word rendered "visitation" in verse 12. Please consult comments on that verse for a discussion of the word. God is the
Bishop of the souls of Christians in the sense that He is the
Overseer of their spiritual welfare. We have the all-seeing eye
of our loving God always upon us, watching tenderly over us
in order that He may nurture our spiritual growth and keep
us from falling into temptations which the world, the flesh,
and Satan are ever placing before us. It is for us to be ever
mindful of God's loving care over us and of the responsibility
we have to obey His Word.

FULLER TRANSLATION

(18) *Household slaves, put yourselves in constant subjection with every fear to your absolute lords and masters; not only to those who are good at heart, but also to those who are against you:* (19) *for this subjection to those who are against you is something which is beyond the ordinary course of what might be expected, and is therefore commendable, namely, when a person because of the conscious sense of his relation to God bears up under pain, suffering unjustly.* (20) *For what sort of fame is it when you fall short of the mark and are pummeled with the fist, you endure this patiently? But if when you are in the habit of doing good and then suffer constantly for it, and this you patiently endure, this is an unusual and not-to-be-expected action, and therefore commendable in the sight of God.* (21) *For to this very thing were you called (namely, to patient endurance in the case of unjust punishment), because Christ also suffered on your behalf, leaving behind for you a model to imitate, in order that by close application you might follow in His footprints;* (22) *who never in a single instance committed a sin, and in whose mouth, after careful scrutiny, there was found not even craftiness;* (23) *who when His heart was being wounded with an accursed sting, and when He was being made the object of harsh rebuke and biting, never retaliated, and who while suffering never threatened, but rather kept on delivering all into the keeping of the One who judges righteously;* (24) *who Himself carried up to the Cross our sins in His own body and offered Himself there as on an altar, doing this in order that we, having died with respect to sin, might live with respect to righteousness, by means of whose bleeding stripes you were healed.* (25) *For you were straying like sheep, but you have turned back to the Shepherd and Overseer of your souls.*

12.

THE ADORNMENT OF THE CHRISTIAN WOMAN
(3:1-7)

Verse one

AFTER singling out as a particular class, Christian house-hold slaves, and exhorting them to be submissive to their masters and to patiently endure unjust punishment, Peter addresses another class of Christians which also was prominent in the early Church, namely, Christian wives who had un-saved husbands. The wife had been saved under the preaching of the gospel, but the husband had remained an unbeliever. These wives were seeking to win their husbands to the Lord Jesus. But they were going about it in the wrong way. The inspired apostle gives them instruction how to win their husbands to the Lord.

The word translated "if" in the Greek text refers to a ful-filled condition. The word "even" in the Greek text is not brought out by the translators. It is, "even if." "Obey not" is the translation of a word which speaks of a state of un-believing disobedience. The word means literally in its verb form, "not to allow one's self to be persuaded." These hus-bands were of that obstinate, non-persuasable type that will not listen to reason. Their wives had often given them the gospel, but they had met it with stiff-necked obstinacy. Peter exhorts them, in view of their husbands' obstinate rejection of the gospel, to stop talking about it, and just live a Christ-like life before them. The husband was to be won to the Lord Jesus not by nagging, but by holy living. Peter says, "that even if any obey not the Word, they may without a word be won." The second occurrence of the word "word" does not have the definite article in the Greek text. These husbands were to be won to the Lord Jesus now without a word from their wives. They knew the gospel. The wife's Christian example, used by God, would do the rest. The word "won" in the Greek text means "to gain, acquire," in the sense of the acquisition of money in James 4:13, here, "to gain" anyone by winning him over to the kingdom of God. "A soul won is a gain to our Lord who bought him, a gain to the one who won him, and a gain to that soul itself." The word "conversation" today refers to the interchange of language between two or more persons. When the A.V. was translated it meant what the Greek word means, "one's behaviour, manner of life." Thus do some English words change their meaning in the course of time. This manner of life included in it submissiveness to their husbands. Both Peter and Paul found it necessary to impress upon the Church that incompatibility of religion did not justify dissolution of marriage. This subjection to their husbands would also be a factor which God could use in winning their husbands.

Verse two

The word "behold" in the Greek text refers to the act of viewing attentively. How carefully the unsaved watch Christians. The word "chaste" in the Greek means not only "chaste" but "pure." The phrase "with fear" is to be understood as referring to the wives, not the husbands. It is their pure manner of life which is coupled with fear that is used of the Lord to gain these husbands. The Greek word "fear" here is used also in Ephesians 5:33 and is there translated "reverence." The word in a connection like this means "to reverence, venerate, to treat with deference or reverential obedience."

Verse three

Peter in verses 1 and 2 exhorts these Christian wives to win their husbands to the Lord by pious living. In this verse, he forbids them to depend upon outward adornment in their effort at gaining their husbands, and not only upon outward adornment as such, but upon worldly adornment, the kind which they wore before they were saved, immodest, gaudy, conspicuous. These women were making the mistake of thinking that if they would dress as the world dressed, that that would please their unsaved husbands, and they would thus be influenced the easier to take the Lord Jesus as Saviour. It is true that they would be pleased, pleased because the appearance of their wives appealed to their totally depraved natures, and pleased because the Christian testimony of their wives was nullified by their appearance. They would say, "What you appear to be speaks so loudly I cannot hear what you are saying." It is not true that that would help win their husbands to the Lord. These wives could hardly have made a greater mistake.

The word "adornment" is the translation of the Greek word *kosmos* which was used in classical Greek to refer to the adornment or the ornaments worn by women. The word in itself refers to an ordered system, namely, a system where order prevails. The word in the Greek opposite in meaning to *kosmos* is *chaos,* which comes into English in the word "chaos," and which means "a rude unformed mass." *Kosmos* is used in the New Testament to refer to the original, perfect creation, a system where order prevailed. Here the word refers to the adornment of the woman, and the genius of the word speaks of the fact that that adornment should be that which is fitting, congruous, not diverse from one's character. That is, the adornment of the Christian woman should be in keeping with what she is as a Christian. She should not be a Christian at heart and her adornment be that of a person of the world.

Then Peter not only forbids worldly adornment, but says that the adornment of the Christian woman should not be mere outward adornment as against that which is from within. This he further develops in verse 4 where the principle is brought out that the adornment of the Christian woman should proceed from within her heart, not be put on from without. But before he enunciates that principle, he speaks of the way these Christian women were adorning themselves, and forbids the same.

First he speaks of the plaiting of the hair. The Greek word refers to an elaborate gathering of the hair into knots. History informs us that the Roman women of that day were addicted to ridiculous extravagance in the adornment of the hair. Juvenal says, "The attendants will vote on the dressing of the hair as if a question of reputation or of life were at stake, so great is the trouble she takes in quest of beauty; with so many tiers does she load, with so many continuous stories does she build up on high her hair. She is as tall as Andromache in front, and behind she is shorter. You would think her another person." Clement of Alexandria comments on this same thing when he says that the women do not even touch their own heads for fear of disturbing their hair, and sleep comes to them with terror lest they should unawares spoil their coiffures. I Timothy 2:9 speaks against the golden combs and nets used for hair ornamentation. What the Word of God forbids the Christian woman is a conspicuous, extravagant, intricate artificiality in the manner of wearing the hair. She must not think that to adopt the latest style of coiffure will give her a better access to someone whom she wishes to lead to the Lord. She will find that it is a hindrance. Why is this worldly artificiality forbidden? It is forbidden because the Holy Spirit does not use the styles of the world in winning a lost soul to the Lord as He seeks to work through the believer. It is forbidden because such an elaborate and worldly display gratifies what the apostle John calls "the lust of the eyes." When a Christian woman's appearance appeals to and gratifies the totally depraved nature of the unsaved person whom she is seeking to win to the Lord, she is feeding that person's appetite for sin instead of appealing to that person's conscience. She is confronting that person with the world, not with the Saviour. Such an artificial display also destroys the personal testimony of the soul winner. *We may be fundamental in our doctrine, and yet defeat the power of the Word we give out by the modernism of our appearance.* It is forbidden because God seeks to glorify Himself in the personality and life of the Christian. He made men in His own image. That image is the ideal medium through which He can reveal Himself. But if that image is marred and distorted by artificiality, it becomes an imperfect medium, and the beauty of the Lord Jesus is hidden beneath a veneer of worldliness.

Then the apostle takes up the matter of the wearing of jewelry. The woman's adornment must not be that of the wearing of gold. As the English translation stands this is an absolute prohibition of the wearing of gold jewelry. But this is not the thought in the Greek text. The word translated "wearing" means literally, "putting around," and here gives the picture of these wives covering their persons with a lavish, conspicuous display of jewelry. The wearing of jewelry is not forbidden the Christian woman, but a gaudy, expensive, elaborate display of the same is, and for the same reasons that made necessary the prohibition of a highly artificial manner of wearing the hair.

Then the Word of God speaks of the putting on of apparel. The word "apparel" here is the translation of the common Greek word referring particularly to outer clothing. The translators of the A.V. caught the meaning of what the apostle was after when they used the word "apparel" instead of "clothing" or "garments." The purpose of clothing is for the protection of the body and for the sake of modesty and good taste. The purpose of apparel is for the adornment of the body. The choice of this word was therefore good, for Peter certainly is not forbidding the wearing of clothing, but the donning of such apparel as these wives were using in an effort to win their husbands to the Lord, clothing that the world wore, immodest, gaudy, conspicuous. Such clothing hides the Lord Jesus who should Himself be conspicuous in the life. Such clothing attracts to itself and to the wearer, whereas the business of a Christian is to let the Lord Jesus be radiated from the life by the Holy Spirit. Paul speaks against this tendency in the words, "Be not conformed to this world" (Rom. 12:2). The Greek word "conformed" refers to the act of a person assuming an outward expression which does not come from within and is therefore not truly representative of his inner character, this expression assumed from the outside and patterned after the world. The English word "masquerade" fits this Greek word exactly. When Christian women adorn themselves in the coiffures of the world, copy the world's lavish and gaudy display of jewelry, and don the apparel of the world, they are masquerading in the garments of the world. They are playing the part of another. They are, in the language of the Greeks, hypocrites, acting the part of another on the stage of life. They dress like the world and act like the world, and the world thinks them to be people of the world. Then when they come with the news of the gospel, their message falls on deaf ears.

Verse four

In verses 1-3, the inspired apostle lays down a two-fold prohibition, first, that the Christian woman must not depend upon outward adornment as she seeks to maintain a Christian testimony, and second, that she must not adorn herself in the habiliments of the world. The manner of wearing the hair must not be highly artificial and in conformity with the latest styles in hair-dress dictated by the fashions of the hour. There must not be a lavish and gaudy display of jewelry. The clothing which she selects must not be conspicuous, immodest, worldly in appearance.

Now Peter comes to the positive part of his subject. He lays down the fundamental principles upon which a Christian woman should act in the matter of adornment. That principle can be stated as follows: The Christian woman should depend upon an adornment that proceeds from within her inner spiritual being and is truly representative of that inner spir-

itual life. The words, "the hidden man of the heart" refer to
the personality of the Christian woman as made beautiful by
the ministry of the Holy Spirit in glorifying the Lord Jesus
and manifesting Him in and through her life. Peter describes
that personality briefly in the case of these wives as a meek
and quiet spirit which is in the sight of God of great price.
The only self-description our Lord ever used of Himself as reported in the Gospels is found in the two words "meek" and
"lowly" (Matt. 11:29). The adornment must be spiritual, not
physical. Personality is after all far more important than
either physical beauty or the adornment which mere clothing
affords. A person ought to be bigger than any consideration of
outward decoration. One can dress up a fence post. If one
finds it necessary to depend upon either physical beauty or
clothing in order to make a favorable impression upon others,
that fact shows that that person realizes his lack of those personal and spiritual qualities that make a virile Christian
character.

The principle to the effect that adornment should proceed
from within and be truly representative of the inner being is
the principle upon which God operates. It is said of God,
"Who coverest thyself with light as with a garment" (Psalm
104:2). But this light comes from the inmost being of God
and is an expression of His intrinsic essence. The light that
caused our Lord's face and garments to shine with a heavenly
radiance in the Transfiguration (Matt. 17:2), came, as the
Greek verb indicates, from His inmost being. Adam and Eve
before they fell into sin were adorned with an enswathement
of glory that was produced from within their inner beings and
was truly representative of their inner spiritual lives. When
they sinned, the power to thus adorn themselves left them, and
finding that their bodies had death and sin and decay in them,
they made clothing to cover up their sin and shame. Our
Lord after His resurrection covered His glorified body with
an enswathement of glory that was produced by the new life
principle motivating His resurrection body. What does a

glorified body have to do with clothing whose purpose it is to cover a mortal body? Had our Lord worn clothing as He appeared to His disciples (Luke 24), they would not have been frightened. His glory covering caused Him to appear for the moment to the disciples as a spirit. When the saints receive their glorified bodies, that power of producing an outward adornment which comes from within and is truly representative of one's inner nature will return, and the saints will shine with the glory of a new life principle motivating their resurrection bodies. The angel Lucifer before he fell was covered with an enswathement of glory, for he was an angel of light. He produced his outward covering from within. When he fell into sin, he became an angel of darkness, that glory covering departed, and he gave expression to the darkness of sin that was true of his inner being. But Paul tells us that Satan has transformed himself into an angel of light (II Cor. 11:13-15). The Greek verb used in this passage speaks of Satan's action of changing his outward expression by assuming, from the outside, an appearance or expression of light. He masquerades as an angel of light. God works upon the same principle in the animal kingdom. The fur-bearing animals produce their beautiful fur from the inside. The plumage of birds is grown from within.

Just so, on the same principle, a Christian woman's adornment should come from within her inner spiritual nature and be truly representative of that nature. Paul in Romans 12:2 (fuller translation) says to the saints, "Stop assuming an outward expression that does not come from and is not representative of your inner being, an expression patterned after the world, but change your outward expression by giving outward expression of your inner being." The chief adornment of the Christian should be the Lord Jesus, manifested in and through the life of the believer. This is the principle upon which the Christian woman should act in adorning herself.

But while the Christian woman must not depend upon adornment put on from the outside to make herself pleasing

in the eyes of others, that does not mean that she is not to dress
with neatness and good taste, or that she should be austere and
drab in her appearance or so plain in her apparel that she is
conspicuous. True Christianity is something joyful, and expresses itself in color and neatness and good taste. It does not
mean that a Christian woman should not pay careful attention to the details of her apparel. That should be one of her
chief concerns. It does mean that in selecting the manner in
which she shall wear her hair, in choosing the jewelry and
clothing she may wish to put on, she should be guided by the
principle that her chief and basic adornment must be the
Lord Jesus, and that whatever she may choose of wearing apparel, of jewelry, and of hair adornment should be in keeping
with the sweetness, simplicity, and purity of the Lord Jesus.
Then the manner in which she wears her hair, the kind and
amount of jewelry she puts on, and the apparel she dons, will
be attractive without attracting from the Lord Jesus, will be
beautiful without detracting from His beauty, will have character without attracting attention to the person herself, will
be apparent but not obtrusive, and will be in keeping with the
sanctifying work of the Holy Spirit in her life. Then the
Lord Jesus will be seen in her life, and even her physical
adornment will reflect Him. This is the ideal God-glorifying
procedure upon the basis of which a Christian woman should
act in the manner of her personal adornment.

Verse five

In this verse, the apostle speaks of another adornment of
the Christian woman, that of subjection to her husband. The
phrase "holy women," should not be interpreted as referring
to some particular and unique class of Old Testament individual with a special halo about her head. These women
concerning whom the apostle is speaking were just ordinary
sinners saved by grace. The word "holy" is the translation of
a Greek word which means literally, "set-apart ones." These
women lived holy lives because they lived separated lives,

separated from the world out from which God had saved
them. It can be done in the days in which we are living. The
word "trusted" is from the Greek word meaning "to hope."
The entire expression in the Greek text describes these women
as those whose hope was directed towards and rested in God.
The Greek word "adorned" is in the imperfect tense which
speaks of action going on in past time. They were accustomed to adorn themselves in that manner. It was a habit
of life with them to adorn themselves with a meek and quiet
spirit, not with the habiliments of the world. Subjection to
their husbands, which Peter defines in verse 6 as obedience to
their husbands, was one of the elements in this adornment.

Verse six

The word "obeyed" is in the constative aorist in Greek
which speaks of an action going on over a long period of time,
looking at it in one single panoramic view. The whole tenor
of Sarah's life was one of obedience to her husband. She
called him "lord." The Greek word translated "lord" is *kurios,*
a word used in various ways. It is the word used in the LXX
as the Greek equivalent of the august title of God "Jehovah." The word was used as a title of the Roman emperors, the
term carrying with it the implication of divinity which was
ascribed to them. It is the word used for the name "Lord,"
when it is applied to the Lord Jesus. It is the word which
the Philippian jailer used when he said, "Sirs, what must I do
to be saved?" It is used in the sentence, "No man can keep on
serving two masters" (Matt. 6:24). The word was used in
secular Greek as a title of honor addressed by subordinates to
their superiors, or as a courteous appellative in the case of persons closely related. In a petition to a Prefect we have, "I became very weak, my lord." In another example we have, "I
entreat you, sir, to hasten to me." The designation is applied
to near relatives, to a father, mother, brother, sister, son, and
in one expression probably to a wife. The apostle John uses

it in his second epistle which he writes to the "elect lady," "lady" being the translation of the feminine form of the word. Sarah used it as a wifely courtesy to her husband, and as a recognition of his authority over her. The word "daughters" is in the Greek text here literally "children." These wives, by adorning themselves as Sarah did, would become her children in the sense that a child is like its mother. They would resemble Sarah and follow her example. The words "as long as ye do well" are the translation of one Greek word which Peter uses and which could also be rendered, "if the whole course of your life is in the doing of good." The Greek word translated "amazement" has in it the idea of "terror." Alford suggests an interpretation of this difficult expression; "As long as the believing wives are doing good, they need not be afraid with any sudden terror of the account which their unbelieving husbands may exact from them."

Verse seven

While the subject matter in this verse does not align itself with the contents of verses 1-6, we are including its interpretation and translation with our consideration of those verses, rather than make a separate heading for it. The word "likewise" goes back to 2:17 where exhortations are addressed generally to all the saints. In 2:18-25, Christian household slaves are addressed, in 3:1-6, Christian wives, and in 3:7, now, Christian husbands. Exhortations to a Christian manner of life are addressed only to the saints. God has no exhortations to the unsaved except to believe on the Lord Jesus Christ. The word "dwell" is the translation of an old verb which referred to domestic association. The word "knowledge" here refers to an intelligent recognition of the marriage relation. The word "honor" is the translation of the same Greek word in 1:19 translated "precious." Christian husbands are to deem the helpmeets which God has given them precious, and are to treat them with honor. The word "giving" is the rendering of a Greek word which means "to assign to, to portion off."

Husbands should keep a special place of honor in their hearts for their wives. They should treat them with special deference, courtesy, respect, and kindness. The word "vessel" is the translation of a Greek word referring to a vessel used in the services of the temple (Mark 11:16), also to household utensils. The English word comes from a Latin word *vasellum,* the diminutive form of *vas,* a vase, the Latin words referring to a receptacle which covers and contains. Thus, the word comes to refer to an instrument whereby something is accomplished. It is used in the latter sense here. The word is used of Paul who is called "a chosen vessel" (Acts 9:15), a chosen instrument of God. The husband is to dwell with the wife, remembering that she is an instrument of God as well as the husband, a child of God to be used by Him to His glory. The husband must ever keep in mind that she is the weaker instrument of the two, not morally or intellectually, but physically. This attitude toward the wife on the part of the husband therefore includes loving consideration of the wife in view of the fact that she is not physically as strong as he is.

The husband should pay due honor to the wife because she is a joint-heir together with him of the grace of life, eternal life, the gift of God. That is, he is ever to remember that Christ died for her as well as for him. Her soul is just as precious in the sight of God as his is. This admonition was especially needed at the time when this letter was written because of the low place in general which was accorded womanhood. History records the fact of the high place accorded womanhood in Macedonia, showing that the woman was not generally held in high esteem nor given that respect, reverence, and honor that her sex demands of the man. Christian husbands today will do well to heed this admonition. The husband is to pay her honor so that their prayers be not hindered. The word "hindered" in the Greek text means literally "to cut in, to interrupt." Failure to give due honor to the wife will result in a cutting in on the efficacy of their united prayer times.

FULLER TRANSLATION

(1) *In like manner wives, put yourselves in subjection to your own husbands, in order that even though certain ones obstinately refuse to be persuaded by the Word and are therefore disobedient to it, they may through the manner of life of the wives, without a word, be gained,* (2) *having viewed attentively your pure manner of life which is accompanied by a reverential obedience;* (3) *whose adornment, let it not be that adornment which is from without and merely external, namely, an elaborate gathering of the hair into knots, and a lavish display of gold ornaments, or the donning of (worldly) apparel,* (4) *but let that adornment be the hidden personality, the heart, standing in as its condition and element, the incorruptible ornament of a meek and quiet disposition, which is in the sight of God very costly.* (5) *For thus formerly also the holy women, the ones whose hope is directed to and rests in God, were accustomed to adorn themselves, putting themselves in subjection to their own husbands,* (6) *as Sarah was wont to render obedience to Abraham, calling him lord, whose children (namely, Sarah's) ye become if the whole course of your life is in the doing of good, and you are not fearing even one bit of terror.* (7) *Husbands, in like manner, let your domestic life with respect to them be governed by the dictates of knowledge, they being the weaker instrument, the feminine, holding in reserve for them particularly, honor as to those who are also fellow-inheritors with you of the grace of life, and this, in order that no (Satanic) inroads be made into your prayers.*

13.

THE BEHAVIOR OF THE PERSECUTED CHRISTIAN
(3:8-17)

Verse eight

THE word "finally" does not indicate the conclusion of the letter, but the conclusion of the exhortations to the various classes. The exhortation, "be ye all of one mind," literally "be ye all likeminded," cannot be pressed to refer to minute details but refers to a unity on the major and important points of Christian doctrine and practice that should be maintained among members of the Body of Christ. The words "having compassion" are the translation of a Greek word from which we get our word "sympathy." The word is made up of two Greek words, one word meaning "to be affected" by something, hence "to feel," that is, to have feelings stirred up within one by some circumstance, the other word meaning "with." The word means therefore, "to have a fellow-feeling." It refers here to the interchange of fellow-feeling in either joy or sorrow. It is "rejoice with them that do rejoice, and weep with them that weep" (Rom. 12:15). The English word "sympathy" refers to the fellow-feeling we should have with those that suffer, and that is the secondary meaning of our Greek word. The primary meaning refers to a fellow-feeling with a brother Christian either in his joys or in his sorrows. It takes as much grace sometimes to rejoice with another saint in the way God has blessed him as it does to sympathize with someone who is in sadness. What a miserable thing this petty jealousy is among the saints. The words "love as brethren" are the translation of an adjective. The idea is, "Be loving

· brethren," or "Be brethren who are loving." The word here does not refer to the love that God produces in our hearts as one of the fruits of the Spirit. It is that human affection and fondness for one another as brother Christians which Peter spoke of in the first occurrence of the word "love" in 1:22.

The word "pitiful" as used here is obsolete English. Today it refers to a person or circumstance that arouses pity in the heart. The translation should be, "full of pity." The Greek word means "tenderhearted." The first century was cold and hard-hearted. Christianity, with its tenderizing influence upon the heart, had not had time nor opportunity yet to make much of an impact upon the callous heart of man. Today we have as a result of its benign influence hospitals, homes for the aged, charities of one sort or another. And yet how callous our hearts are to another's pain. Only the over-flowing love of God and the experience of much suffering in one's own life can fit us to really sympathize with others in the sense of feeling their pain ourselves, thus suffering with them. The word "courteous" is the translation of a Greek word which means "humble-minded, having a modest opinion of one's self."

Verse nine

"Rendering" is literally "giving back." "For" is the translation of a preposition meaning "in exchange for." "Blessing" is not a noun, but a participle, "be constantly blessing." "Thereunto" is literally "into this," that is, "for this very purpose."

Verse ten

The word "will" is a present participle in the Greek speaking of an action going on in present time, literally, " he who is wishing or desiring to be loving life." The idea is, "he who is loving life and wishes to continue to do so." The word "refrain" is the translation of a word which speaks of a natural tendency towards that from which the abstention exhorted is to take place, literally, "Let him stop the tendency of his tongue from evil."

Verse eleven

The word "eschew" came originally from a Norman word "eschever" which means "to shun or avoid." The Greek word means literally, "to lean out from." The word here refers to the act of bending aside from one's path at the approach of evil. The word "ensue" is obsolete. The Greek word means "to pursue."

Verse twelve

The word "over" is literally "upon." The eyes of the Lord are directed in a favorable sense for the good of those that are righteous. "Unto" is literally "into." God's ears are "into" the prayers of the righteous. What a picture of God bending down into the very prayers of His children, earnestly listening to their petitions, eager to answer them and come to the aid of those who pray. We have no far off deity to make propitious. We do not have to plead with God to make Him willing to answer our prayers. He is more desirous of answering them than we are to have them answered.

Verse thirteen

The word "and" is, "seeing that God takes such good care of the righteous," who is he that will harm you? This question was asked in view of the persecution and suffering through which these saints were going. Peter tells them that as a result of their righteous lives and God's care, their blessedness will be such as to turn off all the malice of their persecutors and make their suffering itself to be a joy. The word "followers" is the translation of a Greek word meaning "zealots." The verb means "to burn with zeal, to desire earnestly."

Verse fourteen

The words "but and if ye suffer" are in a construction in Greek which refers to a rare thing, a possible but not a probable happening. The idea is, "if matters in spite of the prophetic note of victory in verse 13 should come to actual suffering for righteousness' sake." Alford translates, "If ye chance to suffer." The word "happy" is the translation of a Greek word which means "prosperous." That is, the spiritual state of those who suffer persecution because of their righteous lives is prosperous, spiritually prosperous. The words "be not afraid of their terror" involve what is called a cognate accusative, where the idea in the object of the verb is the same as that in the verb. Literally it is: "Be not affected with fear by the fear which they strive to inspire in your heart." The word "troubled" in the Greek means "to disturb, be agitated."

Verse fifteen

The word "sanctify" is the translation of a Greek word meaning "to set apart." It was used in the pagan Greek religions of the act of setting apart a building as a temple, thus designating it as religious in character, to be used for religious purposes. The word "God" is a rejected reading and "Christ" appears in the best texts. The exhortation is to set apart Christ as Lord in the heart. The word "Lord" is the translation of *kurios,* here referring to Christ as the Jehovah of the Old Testament. The word "Christ" is the English spelling of the Greek word *christos,* which in turn is the Greek translation of the Hebrew word meaning "The Anointed One," which latter is a designation of the Jewish Messiah. Peter was exhorting these Jews to set apart their Messiah, the Lord Jesus, as Jehovah, Very God, in their hearts, giving first place to Him in obedience of life. The word *kurios* also has the idea of "master" in it. Thus, the second Person of the Triune God was to be lord and master of their lives. He was to be their resource and defender when persecution came.

Not only were these Christian Jews to find a refuge in Christ Jesus as they set Him apart as Lord of their lives, but they were to be ready to give an answer to these persecutors who attacked them and the Word of God which they believed. The words "give an answer" are the translation of a Greek word used as a legal term in the courts. It means literally "to talk off from," and was used of an attorney who talked his client off from a charge preferred against him. He presented a verbal defense. The exhortation is to Christians to talk the Bible off from the charges preferred against it, thus presenting for it a verbal defense. Today, Modernism has preferred charges against the Word of God, has placed it in the dungeons of the destructive critic's inquisition, and has charged it with gross errors, and with being man-made. It is not allowed to speak for itself except through the prosecuting attorney, the destructive critic. But those who believe in a whole Bible, rather than a Bible full of holes, are admonished not to remain silent in the face of this attack by Modernism, but to defend the Bible against these false charges by presenting a verbal defense for it, refuting the statements of the destructive critic. Such a great classical Greek scholar as Professor John A. Scott, Ph.D., LL.D., in his excellent defense of the historical accuracy of the Gospels,[1] writing in a context of the discovery of ancient manuscripts says, "So far as I know, not a single discovery has ever confirmed the conclusions of destructive criticism either in classical or biblical literature." This defense of the Bible, Peter cautions us, must be conducted in a spirit of meekness and fear. The Christian apologist who defends the Faith once for all delivered to the saints, must not deal with the opposition in a high-handed, domineering way. He must follow in the footsteps of the One who said of Himself, "I am meek and lowly in heart." He must defend the Faith with fear in his heart. "This fear is self-distrust; it is tenderness of conscience; it is vigilance against temptation; it is the fear which inspiration opposes

---

1. *We Would Know Jesus*, by John A. Scott.

to high-mindedness in the admonition, 'be not highminded
but fear.' It is taking heed lest we fall; it is a constant apprehension of the deceitfulness of the heart, and of the insidiousness and power of inward corruption. It is the caution and
circumspection which timidly shrinks from whatever would
offend and dishonor God and the Saviour" (WARDLAW).

Verse sixteen

But in addition to meekness and fear, the defender of the
Faith must have a good conscience. Vincent translates, "having a conscience good or unimpaired." The words "that
whereas they speak evil of you" can be rendered a little more
accurately, "that in the matter in which ye are spoken against,"
that is, in the matter of Christianity and one's testimony to it
by life and word, these critics of the Bible may be put to
shame in that their misrepresentation of Christians and of
Christianity will be shown to be wrong. The words "falsely
accuse" are very strong in the Greek, namely, "to spitefully
abuse, to insult, to traduce." The words "good conversation"
refer to the Christian behavior of the recipients of this letter, the word "conversation" having the meaning of "manner of life or behavior" when the A.V. was translated. Today
of course it means "talk." This behavior was in Christ in the
sense that He was the center and the circumference of all their
thoughts, words, and deeds.

Verse seventeen

Peter informs the recipients of this letter that it is better to
suffer for doing good than to suffer for wrong-doing. The
words, "if the will of God be so," do not present a proba-
bility, but only a possibility in the Greek, "if perchance the
will of God should so will," that is, for the Christian to suffer
for doing well.

FULLER TRANSLATION

(8) *Now, to come to a conclusion. Be all of you like-minded. Have fellow-feeling for one another. Be brethren who are loving. Be tenderhearted. Be humbleminded,* (9) *not giving back evil in exchange for evil, or railing in exchange for railing, but instead on the contrary, be constantly blessing, since for this very purpose you were called, that you might inherit a blessing.* (10) *For he who desires to be loving life and to see good days, let him stop the natural tendency of his tongue towards evil, and the natural tendency of his lips to the end that they speak no craftiness,* (11) *but let him rather at once and once for all turn away from evil and let him do good. Let him seek peace and pursue it,* (12) *because the Lord's eyes are directed in a favorable attitude towards the righteous, and His ears are inclined into their petitions, but the Lord's face is against those who practice evil things.* (13) *And who is he that will do you evil if you become zealots of the good?* (14) *But if even you should perchance suffer for the sake of righteousness, (you are spiritually) prosperous ones. Moreover, do not be affected with fear by the fear which they strive to inspire in you, neither become agitated,* (15) *but set apart Christ as Lord in your hearts, always being those who are ready to present a verbal defense to everyone who asks you for a logical explanation concerning the hope which is in all of you, but doing this with meekness and fear,* (16) *having a conscience unimpaired, in order that in the very thing in which they defame you, they may be put to shame, those who spitefully abuse, insult, and traduce your good behavior which is in Christ;* (17) *for it is better when doing good, if perchance it be the will of God, that ye be suffering, rather than when doing evil.*

14.

THE REWARD OF SUFFERING FOR WELL DOING
(3:18-22)

Verse eighteen

PETER, in verse 17, stated that it was better to suffer for well-doing than for evil-doing. In verses 18-22 he shows that blessing always follows suffering for well-doing. He says that Christ also suffered for well-doing when He died on the Cross in order to make a way of salvation for sinful humanity (v. 18), that because He suffered for well-doing He was raised from the dead (v. 21) and given the place of glory and honor (v. 22). Paul presents the same idea in Philippians 2:5-11. When speaking of His death on the Cross in verse 18, and His resurrection and position of honor and glory in verses 21, 22, the inspired apostle also gives the reader some facts concerning our Lord between His death on the Cross and His resurrection from the tomb in verses 18b-20. Thus Peter encourages these Jewish Christians in their sufferings which they incurred by the doing of good, for Christ's example made it clear to them that they also would receive blessing and reward for suffering when doing good. The word "for" is the translation of a Greek conjunction which means "because." The resurrection of Christ and His consequent glorification in view of His suffering for sinners are presented as proof of the fact that suffering for well-doing on the part of Christians is also followed by blessing and reward in their lives.

The word "suffered" is not in the best Greek texts, instead, the word "died." However, the thought is not changed since

Christ's death involved suffering. Peter says that Christ's death, thus His sufferings, were in relation to sin, and that the sufferings of these Christian Jews were in relation to sin. His sufferings were vicarious. That is, He, the innocent One, died in behalf of the guilty. Our sufferings are not vicarious but merely a natural consequence upon our doing of the right. The words "just" and "unjust" are not preceded by the definite article in the Greek text, which is indicative of the fact that the writer is emphasizing quality or nature. The idea is, "a just Person in character in behalf of unjust persons in character."

Peter says that our Lord died in order that He might bring us to God. The word "God" is preceded by the article in the Greek, showing that the apostle is speaking here of God the Father. The word "bring" in the Greek text means literally "to lead to." It was a technical word used of one who gained an audience at court for another. He brought his friend into the good graces of the reigning monarch. Just so, our Lord Jesus by dying on the Cross and paying for our sins, satisfied the just penalty of the broken law which we incurred by our disobedience, and removed for us that which barred our access to God. Thus as lost sinners receive Him as their Saviour, they are led into the presence of God the Father by God the Son, dressed in a righteousness, Christ Jesus Himself who brings us into the place of the unlimited favor of God. The word *entree* is the ideal word here which exactly reproduces the thought in the Greek. The Lord Jesus has provided for lost sinners an entree into the presence of God. Have you, dear reader, received Him as your Saviour, and as a consequence been led into the presence of the God of all grace?

In the words, "being put to death in the flesh, but quickened by the Spirit," Peter introduces the facts which he wishes his readers to know concerning our Lord which took place between His death on the Cross (v. 18) and His resurrection from the tomb (v. 21). The words, "being put to death," are an aorist participle in the Greek text, speaking of a past fact,

namely, "having been put to death." The words, "in the
flesh," are the translation of one word in Greek, *sarki,* the
word for flesh here referring to the physical body and human
existence of our Lord. The dative case is used by the writer.
The particular classification of the dative here is the dative
of respect. That is, our Lord was put to death with respect
to the flesh. The definite article is absent, its absence emphasizing character. The character of this death is in the apostle's
mind. The word "flesh" defines the word "death." Peter
was speaking of the physical death of our Lord on the Cross.

The words, "but quickened by the Spirit," are set in contrast to the words, "having been put to death with respect to
the flesh." The things set in contrast are first, the act of
putting to death which is contrasted to the act of quickening,
and second, the flesh which is contrasted to the Spirit. The
word "quickened" is the translation of *zoopoietheis,* which is
made up of the word *poieo* meaning "to make" and *zoe,*
which means "alive." The word does not mean "to energize,"
but "to make alive." The Greek word meaning "to energize"
is *energeo.* But to make something alive presupposes a condition of death. A living person may be energized, but only
a dead person can be made alive. The opposite of death is
life. We have therefore a contrast between two things, death
and life, which are logical opposites of one another.

In the same way, the words "flesh" and "Spirit" are contrasted and are logical opposites. The word translated
"Spirit," *pneumati,* is in the same case and classification as
the word for "flesh," *sarki.* But the Holy Spirit is not a
logical contrast to the human body of our Lord. It is the
human spirit of our Lord that is set over against His human
body. It is true that our Lord was raised from the dead by
the power of the Holy Spirit, and that is taught by Paul in
Romans 8:11. But Peter is not teaching that truth here. He
maintains the perfect contrast between our Lord's human
body and His human spirit. The translators of the A.V. have
capitalized the word "spirit," making it refer to the Holy

Spirit. But the following considerations will show that they had no textual basis for doing so. In the first place, the three oldest and best manuscripts we have, the Vaticanus and the Sinaiticus, fourth century, and the Alexandrinus of the fifth, are in capital letters entirely. The Chester Beatty manuscript, third century, does not contain the portion of Scripture we are studying. Eberhard Nestle in his text which is the resultant of a collation of three of the principal recensions of the Greek Testament appearing in the latter half of the nineteenth century, Tischendorf, 1869-1872, Westcott and Hort, 1881-1895, and Bernhard Weiss, 1894-1900, capitalizes the word "spirit" when the word is used to designate the third Person of the Triune God. But he has no manuscript evidence for doing this. With him it is a pure matter of interpretation. Every word of his Greek text which appeared in the originals is the inspired Word of God, but the capitalization is not inspired. The word "spirit" in I Peter 3:18 is not capitalized in Nestle's text, which indicates that he thought that the word referred, not to the Holy Spirit but to the human spirit of the Lord Jesus. But this again is a textual critic's interpretation. All of which goes to say that the present writer has a perfect right to write the word "spirit" in the passage in question without capitalization if he thinks that a careful exegesis of its context, based upon the rules of Greek grammar, warrants him in doing so. The problem is therefore purely one of interpretation and not at all of textual evidence. The translation reads, "having in fact been put to death with respect to the flesh, but made alive with respect to the spirit." That preserves the balance in which the apostle contrasts the physical death of our Lord with the fact that His human spirit was made alive. But how are we to understand this latter?

To make alive Christ's human spirit presupposes the death of that human spirit. Our Lord on Calvary's Cross cried, "My God, my God, why hast thou forsaken me?" (Matt. 27:46). The Greek word translated "forsaken" means "to abandon, desert, leave in straits, leave helpless, leave destitute, leave in the lurch, let one down." The cry was addressed to the two other members of the Triune God. God the Father had abandoned and deserted Him. This is clearly seen by the fact that our Lord asks the question and also in that no answer to our Lord's question comes from the Father. The fellowship had been broken. Our Lord's prayer was unanswered. This unanswered prayer was predicted in type in Leviticus 5:11 where an offerer too poor to bring a blood offering could bring the tenth part of an ephah of fine flour, just enough to bake one day's supply of bread, the giving up of the flour typifying the giving up of life, thus pointing to our Lord's death. But he was forbidden to include frankincense with the flour. Frankincense is a type of answered prayer. Flour without frankincense speaks of our Lord's death and His unanswered prayer. The sin of man had been laid on God the Son, and He was made a curse for us.

The question, "Why hast thou left Me in straits, left Me helpless, destitute, in the lurch, why hast thou let Me down?" was also addressed to God the Holy Spirit. The same necessity which caused God the Father to abandon God the Son caused the Holy Spirit to do the same. Our Lord in His incarnation had a human body (Matt. 26:26), a human soul (John 12:27), and a human spirit (Luke 23:46). That human spirit during our Lord's earthly existence was energized by the Holy Spirit, with the result that every prayer our Lord uttered, every word He spoke, every miracle He performed, the sinless wonderful life He lived, was in dependence upon and in the energy of the Holy Spirit, so that He was able to offer Himself at the Cross without spot to become the sacrifice that God would accept as the atonement for sin (Heb. 9:14, "who through the eternal Spirit offered himself without spot to God"). But now, in the hour of His direst need, the Holy Spirit left Him helpless and in the lurch. He abandoned the Son just as surely as did God the Father. This is predicted in type in Leviticus 5:11 where the offerer is forbidden to include oil in the flour. Oil is a type of the Holy Spirit. No oil in the flour speaks of the withdrawal of the Holy Spirit's sustaining presence while our Lord was suffering on the Cross. He ceased keeping alive in divine life the human spirit of our Lord. That human spirit, sinless though it was and continued to be, was dead in that the life-giving power of the Holy Spirit ceased to energize it. Psalm 22 is thought with good reason to have been uttered on the Cross by our Lord. In verses 1-13, our Lord describes His heart sufferings, in verses 14-18, His physical sufferings. In verses 19-31 we have His prayer for resurrection. It was while our Lord was uttering the words found in verses 1-18 that His human spirit was devoid of the life-giving ministry of the Holy Spirit. And this latter was a matter of hours, for our Lord cried out to God in the day time, 9-12 o'clock in the morning, and in the night season, 12-3 in the afternoon, and God the Father would not hear Him.

But then when He prayed that He might be raised from the dead, the Holy Spirit had already returned to make alive again His human spirit, for that prayer was answered. Sin had been paid for. The atonement was looked upon as complete. The fellowship between God the Father and God the Son was restored before the Son died on the Cross. This is what Peter has reference to when he says, "but made alive with reference to the spirit."

Verse nineteen

The words "by which" in the Greek text are *en hoi,* a preposition and a relative pronoun, the latter either in the locative or the instrumental cases, since the preposition is used with both cases. The pronoun is either masculine or neuter, and there being a neuter noun "spirit" immediately preceding it, the word "which" according to the rules of Greek grammar, refers back to the word "spirit." One could translate either "in which spirit," or "by means of which spirit." The word "went" is a translation of *poreuomai,* a word that is used of one travelling, going on a journey. The translation reads now, "in which (human) spirit having proceeded," or, "by means of which human spirit having proceeded." This speaks of our Lord in His disembodied state after He had spoken the words, "Into thy hands I commend my spirit" (Luke 23:46). His human body was laid in Joseph's tomb, but He as the Man Christ Jesus, possessing His human soul and human spirit, departed this life. It is clear that our Lord as the Man Christ Jesus went to the place of the departed dead called in the Old Testament "sheol" and in the New Testament, "hell" (Acts 2:27), the word "hell" being the translation of the Greek word "Hades."[1] But Peter is not speaking of that here. Peter says "in which" or "by means of which (human) spirit also having proceeded, He preached unto the spirits in prison." The word "also" speaks of the fact that it was in His human spirit as made alive by the Holy Spirit that our Lord proceeded.

The question before us now is, "Who are these spirits?" They cannot be human beings, for a careful study of the Greek word "spirit" *pneuma* in the Greek New Testament will reveal the fact that in no place is the word used as a designation of a human being when the writer has in mind a human being considered as a free moral agent in a distinctive category or class of created beings. The word is used where a human being is said to have a spirit, referring to that part of a person which enables him to have God-consciousness and which constitutes him a religious being (Luke 1:47). It is used of the disembodied state of human beings in the phrase, "the spirits of just men made perfect" (Heb. 12:23). But in this latter phrase, it does not designate the human being as a class, distinct in the order of created beings, but speaks of the disembodied state of that human being. Our Lord in His glorified humanity is spoken of as "a quickening spirit" (I Cor. 15:45). This again refers not to Him as an individual but to His new position and condition resultant

---

1. *Treasures*, pp. 44-47.

upon His resurrection. The context speaks of the natural body and the spiritual body, the body before death, and the resurrected body. It is the glorified state of our Lord which was in Paul's mind as he wrote the words "a quickening spirit." Observe with what meticulous care the inspired writer of the letter to the Hebrews uses the word *pneuma* in 12:23. He uses the word as a designation of angels in 1:7, 14. In 12:22 he uses the word "angels" when referring to the myriads of heavenly beings, and in connection with them he speaks of the saints in heaven in the words "spirits of just men made perfect." He seems to feel that the word *pneuma* here needs some qualifying phrase to indicate to the reader that he is not referring to a created intelligence as such and considered as belonging to a distinct category, but to saints in heaven who were spirits only in the sense that they as human beings are temporarily without their physical bodies. It would seem therefore that if the word "spirits" *pneuma* in I Peter 3:18 referred to human beings in their disembodied state, the apostle Peter, inspired by the same Holy Spirit in His work of guiding the Bible writers as they wrote down in God-chosen words the truth of God, would have also qualified the word.

The word *pneuma* is used as a designation of just two classes of free moral agents in the New Testament, of angels (Heb. 1:7, 14), and of demons (Matt. 8:16; Luke 10:17, 20), the word "devils" being the translation of *daimonion* in the A.V., but should be "demons," the word "devil" being the correct translation of *diabolos,* a name of Satan.[1] We must be careful to differentiate angels from demons. Acts 23:8, 9, is enough to show us that the Jews made a difference between them. One thing that clearly distinguishes them in the New Testament is the fact that demons take up their residence in the physical bodies of men and women, and have no rest until they do so (Matt. 12:43-45). This clearly infers that at one time they had physical bodies, and being deprived of them

---

1. *Nuggets,* p. 104.

through some judgment of God, they try to satisfy their innate desire for a physical existence in that way. This is not true of angels.

But are the spirits of our First Peter passage angels or demons? Peter tells us that these spirits were in prison. There are just two prisons in the unseen world where evil spirits are confined, Tartarus (II Peter 2:4, "hell" *tartarosas*) where fallen angels are kept; and the Bottomless Pit (Rev. 9:1-12). When our Lord was about to cast out the demons from the maniac of Gadara, they besought Him not to cast them into the deep, the *abusson* (Luke 8:31). The words "bottomless pit" of Revelation 9:1 are literally "the well of the *abusson*," same Greek word as used in Luke 8:31, which fixes the Bottomless Pit as the prison house of demons. To which place did our Lord go and preach? Peter in his first epistle (3:19, 20) and in his second epistle (2:4, 5) links spirits and angels with the flood and states that they sinned at that time. The inference should be clear that he is referring to the same beings, for Hebrews uses the words "angels" and "spirits" as designating the same created beings, and Peter is just following the practice of other inspired writers.

Our Lord therefore, between His death on the Cross and His resurrection from Joseph's tomb, preached to the fallen angels in Tartarus. But what did He preach to them? The word translated "preached" here is *kerusso*. The word was used in secular Greek of an official announcement or proclamation made by a representative of a government. The word in itself does not indicate the content of the message. A qualifying phrase must be used for that purpose. In the New Testament, the word is used either with a qualifying phrase such as "the gospel" (Mark 16:15), or the contents of the proclamation are given as in Revelation 5:2, or it is used alone without the contents of the message being given as in Romans 10:15. Thus, one cannot say that our Lord preached the gospel to these fallen angels. There is a distinct word used in the Greek New Testament which means "to preach the gospel," *euaggelizomai*. In Luke 4:18 we have, "to preach the gospel to the poor," where the words, "preach the gospel" are the translation of the one word *euaggelizomai*. The word is made up of *aggello* "to bring a message," and *eu* "well" or "good," thus, "a message of good," thus, "to bring good news." The word "gospel" means "good news." But this word is not used here. Our Lord made an official proclamation to these fallen angels. It was not the gospel. Angels are not included among those for whom Christ died. Hebrews 2:16 says, "For verily He took not hold of angels: but He took hold of the seed of Abraham." In perfect righteousness, God in justice passed by fallen angels, and in infinite mercy, procured for fallen man a salvation at Calvary, purchased by His own precious blood (Acts 20:28). As to a suggestion regarding the possible content of the proclamation, that must await our treatment of the subject concerning the nature of the disobedience of these fallen angels.

Verse twenty

The sin of these angels was committed just previous to the flood. We have established the fact by a study of the usage of the word *pneuma*, translated in 3:19 "spirits," that Peter is referring here to angels. He states that they were disobedient at the time of the flood. In his second letter (2:4) he speaks of "angels that sinned," and there is no good reason to think that he is referring to a different group of angels from that to which he has reference in 3:19 of his first letter. The connective "and" of 2:4 (second letter) associates the fact that God did not spare the fallen angels with the fact that He did not spare the antediluvian world but saved Noah, thus making clear that these angels are those mentioned in 3:19 of his first letter. These angels have been cast down to hell, the A.V. has it. The word "hell" is here the translation of the Greek word *Tartarosas*, the English spelling being "Tartarus." In the Book of Enoch 22:2, Gehenna is said to be the place of dead apostate Jews, and Tartarus, of fallen angels.

The Greek poet Homer uses the term "Hades" as the place for dead men, and "Tartarus," a murky abyss beneath Hades, for fallen immortals. Peter uses the word in agreement with the Book of Enoch and with Greek mythology, because he is speaking of fallen angels, not men.

Jude in verses 6 and 7 speaks of "the angels which kept not their first estate." The words "first estate" are from the Greek word *arche* which speaks of office and dignity. The word means "the first in order of importance, honor, or position." The word speaks here of the exalted position of angels in heaven, in contradistinction to the lower place occupied by the earth dwellers. This high position and condition, these angels left, which means that they descended to a lower position and condition. In doing that they sinned. Jude refers to the same angels of which Peter speaks. The Book of Enoch 12:4 uses *arche* of the Watchers (angels) who have abandoned the high heaven and the holy eternal place and have defiled themselves with women.

After informing his readers that they have been reserved in everlasting chains under darkness, the murky abyss designated "Tartarus" by Peter, Jude likens the sin of these angels to the sin of Sodom, Gomorrah, and the cities around them. The words "even as" are the translation of an adverb which means literally "like as, in the same manner as." The sin of these angels was of the same character as that committed by the inhabitants of the cities mentioned in verse 7.

The words "in like manner" of verse 7 cannot be construed with the words "and the cities about them," thus confining the sin of fornication to Sodom and Gomorrah and the cities about them. The words "in like manner" do not present a likeness between Sodom and the cities about them. *Expositor's Greek Testament* classifies the words "in like manner" as an adverbial accusative. This means that this phrase is to be construed with the verb translated "giving themselves over to fornication," not with the words "and the cities about them." Therefore the punctuation in the A.V. should be, "Even as Sodom and Gomorrah and the cities about them, in

like manner giving themselves over to fornication." These
words are so punctuated in the Greek text of Eberhard Nestle.
Punctuation in the extant Greek manuscripts is not inspired.
The punctuation of the textual critic is based upon the Greek
grammar involved. This means that the comparison is between the angels of verse 6 and the cities of verse 7. This
interpretation must be conclusive, all opinions to the contrary notwithstanding, for it is based upon the rules of Greek
grammar. The sin in both cases is said to be fornication.
We have the definite statement of Scripture therefore that
the sin of the fallen angels was fornication. *Expositor's* in
commenting on this passage says, "Like them, the fallen
angels." Alford uses the phrase "in like manner to the
angels." This fornication was in character the "going after
strange flesh." The word "strange" is the translation of the
Greek word *heteros* which means "another of a different
kind." In committing this sin of fornication, the angels
transgressed the limits of their own kind and invaded the
realm of another order of being. The sin of Sodom was the
transgressing of the male beyond the limitations imposed by
God (Rom. 1:27). *Expositor's* says in the explanation of the
phrase "going after strange flesh," "In the case of angels the
forbidden flesh (lit. 'other than appointed by God') refers to
the intercourse with women, in the case of Sodom, to the
departure from the natural use" (Rom. 1:27). Alford says
of the same phrase, "It was a departure from the appointed
course of nature and seeking after that which is unnatural,
to other flesh than that appointed by God for the fulfillment
of natural desire." Justin Martyr speaks of the angels who
violated the *taxin* of women by intercourse with them. The
word *taxin* is used in the LXX when speaking of the priestly
order (A.V.) of Melchisedec. The word "order" is used there
to refer to a distinct class or kind of priesthood. Justin
Martyr uses the word to speak of the distinct class in which
women belong, that of the human race as distinct from
angels as a class or order of being. He uses the word *parabaino*
which means "to step beyond, to transgress," when describing

the act of these angels in their act of fornication with these women. It was a mingling of two different orders of beings.

These fallen angels and their sin of committing fornication with women of the human race is spoken of also in Genesis 6:1-4 in the words, "The sons of God saw the daughters of men that they were fair; and they took them wives of all which they chose." The expression "sons of God" is used in only three other places in the Old Testament, Job 1:6, 2:1, and 38:7. In the first two texts, Satan, a fallen angel, is said to have come *also* among the sons of God who presented themselves before the Lord, the clear inference being that the latter were also angels, although unfallen ones. In 38:7 the sons of God are said to have shouted for joy when they saw the universe spring into existence. It should be clear that these are also angels. In every case the word "God" is *Elohim,* the name of God as Creator. The book of Job is probably the oldest of the Bible books, having been written before the giving of the Mosaic law, for it would have been impossible in a discussion covering the whole field of sin, to avoid any reference to that law had it been known. If this is the case, then Moses was just following the terminology used by the inspired author of Job when speaking of angels as sons of God. In the expression "sons of the living God" of Hosea 1:10, the distinctive word for God is *El,* meaning "The Mighty One." The fact that Paul and John both use the expression, "sons of God," to designate believers in this age, has no bearing upon our discussion since Moses is not likely to have used New Testament terms. There is no good reason to doubt that Moses is referring to angels in our Genesis passage.

This was the prevailing view of the passage in the ancient synagogue of the Jews. Josephus, Jewish historian of the first century, speaks of the sons of God of Genesis 6 as angels, and in such a way as to indicate that that was the commonly accepted interpretation in his day. It was the view held by Christian theologians for the first three or four centuries of the Church. Dr. James M. Gray in his book *Spiritism and the Fallen Angels* says, "There is reason to believe it would not have been changed in the latter case, had it not been for certain erroneous opinions and practices of Christendom."

One of these was angel worship which tended to remove everything that might shake confidence in the holiness of angels or mar the gratification which their worship afforded. The other was celibacy. To interpret the Genesis passage as referring to human "sons of God" instead of angelic "sons of God" would give an excuse for monkish transgressions occasioned by the fact that these celibates chafed at their self-imposed restrictions.

It remains to suggest the possible purpose of Satan in this angelic inroad into the human race. Dr. Gray speaking of the term "sons of God" as used to designate angels says, "Moreover if it were so used, it would carry with it a confounding of two distinct orders of creatures and the production of a mixed race, partly human, partly super-human, which would be just such a derangement of the divine plan as to warrant that which occurred, namely, the almost total extermination of all who were upon the earth." Now, connecting this with the fact that our Lord after His death on the Cross, went to Tartarus and made a proclamation to these fallen angels, we suggest that the probable purpose of the angelic apostasy so far as Satan was concerned was the derangement of the divine plan of the incarnation and substitutionary atonement of the Son of God, for if his purpose had succeeded, God would not have incarnated Himself in a race part angel and part man. The last Adam was to be God the Son come in a human incarnation to answer in His humanity to the humanity of the first Adam. The action of God in completely exterminating the race and saving Noah and his family prevented the spread of this unlawful mingling of angelic and human natures, and allowed the incarnation to take place. The proclamation was probably to the effect that, in the incarnation and the Cross, God had defeated the scheme of Satan to defeat His purpose. It would therefore be a proclamation of victory. For a complete treatment of this subject see *Spiritism and the Fallen Angels* by Dr. James M. Gray.

The principal objection to the view that the fallen angels committed fornication with evil women of the human race is that an angel is altogether spiritual and immaterial, and that such a thing is therefore impossible. To meet this objection, Dr. Gray offers the following four points: First, that could not change the fact that the sons of God took wives of the daughters of men, and that the phrase "sons of God" is used everywhere in the Old Testament of angels, not of men. He says: "Faith does not wait to learn the possibility of a thing before it believes it. It believes it on the evidence presented, assuming its possibility until the opposite is shown." Second, no one is qualified to say just what angelic nature may be, because no one knows. Angels have appeared in human form and have partaken of food like human beings. Third, angels, even fallen angels, can work miracles, for instance, Satan assuming the body of a serpent in Eden. Angels do not possess creative powers, but they may be able to so combine existing elements as to form for themselves bodies like that of human beings. Fourth, human bodies have been possessed by demons who are spiritual intelligences similar to but not of the same category as angels. The large physical proportions, the superhuman strength, and evil dispositions of the offspring of the union between fallen angels and evil women, the giants, men of renown of Genesis 6:5, would be accounted for by the power thus imparted by the former.

As to the interpretation which holds that the sons of God were the men of the righteous line of Seth, and the daughters of men, the women of the evil line of Cain, by what law of exegesis can that be sustained? It is pure eisegesis (reading into the text what is not there) to say that the words "daughters of men" refer to the women in the line of Cain. By what right can one limit the word "men" to a separate portion of the human race, when the word is race-wide in its significance, and then go a step further and single it out as a distinctive part of the human race, the Cainitic line? Then as to the term "sons of God." In the New Testament, the word "son" *huios* is used as a designation of a child of God in this dispensation of grace. But Moses was unlikely to be using New Testament terms. And who would be prepared to say that all men of the line of Seth were saved and sons of God in that sense, and none of the men of the line of Cain? And the question might be asked as to whether godly men would enter into such marriages, and obtain a plurality of wives, and do so by exercising force? And would the union of the lines of Seth and Cain produce beings of superhuman character and strength? The interpretation falls by its own weight.

Peter speaks of the ark "wherein few, that is, eight souls were saved by water." The words "were saved" are literally in the Greek, "were brought safely through." The preposition "by" is from *dia*, a preposition of intermediate agency. That is, the souls in the ark were brought safely through the time of the flood by the intermediate agency of water. While it is true that it was the ark that saved them, yet Peter is not teaching that here. He says the waters of the flood saved them. They buoyed up the ark above their own death-dealing powers and saved those inside the ark. The very waters that were death to the rest of the human race were life to the inmates of the ark. The former were drowned because they were not rightly related to the waters. The latter were saved because they were correctly adjusted to them. The righteousness of God that banishes forever from His presence those who reject it because they refuse to place their faith in the Saviour, saves and keeps saved forever those who accept it at the hands of the God who perfectly satisfied His just law which we broke, by stepping down from His judgment throne to take upon Himself our sin and penalty, thus satisfying His justice and making possible the righteous bestowal of His mercy. Dear reader, what is your relationship to this righteousness? Are you trusting in your own righteousness which according to Isaiah 64:6 is filthy rags in God's sight, or are you standing in a perfect righteousness, Jesus Christ Himself, through faith in His Blood?

Verse twenty-one

The words "the like figure" are in the Greek *ho antitupon*. The question as to whether the word "figure" refers back to the word "ark" or the word "water," is easily settled by the Greek grammar involved in this expression, for the relative pronoun *ho* is neuter, the word "ark" is feminine, and the word "water" neuter. The relative pronoun agrees with its antecedent in gender. Therefore the word "figure" which is neuter and construed grammatically with the pronoun *ho*, goes back to the word "water." The word "figure" is the translation of *antitupon* which means "the counterpart of reality." The Greek word "baptism" is in apposition with the word "figure." Our translation so far reads, "Which (water) also (as a) counterpart now saves you, (namely) baptism." Water baptism is clearly in the apostle's mind, not the baptism by the Holy Spirit, for he speaks of the waters of the flood as saving the inmates of the ark, and in this verse, of baptism saving believers. But he says that it saves them only as a counterpart. That is, water baptism is the counterpart of the reality, salvation. It can only save as a counterpart, not actually. The Old Testament sacrifices were counterparts of the reality, the Lord Jesus. They did not actually save the believer, only in type. It is not argued here that these sacrifices are analagous to Christian water baptism. The author is merely using them as an illustration of the use of the word "counterpart." So water baptism only saves the believer in type. The Old Testament Jew was saved before he brought the offering. That offering was only his outward testimony that he was placing his faith in the Lamb of God of whom these sacrifices were a type. The moment he conceived in his heart that he would bring his offering to the Tabernacle, his faith leaped the centuries to the time when God would offer the Sacrifice that would pay for his sin. Our Lord said, "Abraham rejoiced to see my day: and he saw it, and was glad" (John 8:56). The act of bringing the sacrifice was his outward expression and testimony of his inward faith. Water baptism is the outward testimony of the believer's inward faith. The person is saved the moment he places his faith in the Lord Jesus. Water baptism is his visible testimony to his faith and the salvation he was given in answer to that faith.

Peter is careful to inform his readers that he is not teaching baptismal regeneration, namely, that a person who submits to baptism is thereby regenerated, for he says, "not the putting away of the filth of the flesh." Baptism, Peter explains, does not wash away the filth of the flesh, either in a literal sense as a bath for the body, nor in a metaphorical sense as a cleansing for the soul. No ceremonies really affect the conscience. But he defines what he means by salvation, in the words "the answer of a good conscience toward God," and he explains how this is accomplished, namely "by the resurrection of Jesus Christ" in that the believing sinner is identified with Him in that resurrection.

FULLER TRANSLATION

(18) *Because Christ also died once for all in relation to sins, a just One on behalf of unjust ones, in order that He might provide you with an entree into the presence of God, having in fact been put to death with respect to the flesh, but made alive with respect to the spirit,* (19) *in which (human spirit) also proceeding, He made proclamation to the spirits in prison* (20) *who were at one time rebels when the long-suffering of God waited out to the end in the days of Noah while the ark was being made ready; in which eight souls were brought safely through by means of the intermediate agency of water,* (21) *which (water) as a counterpart now saves you, (namely) baptism; not a putting off of filth of flesh, but the witness of a good conscience toward God, through the resurrection of Jesus Christ* (22) *who is at the right hand of God, having proceeded into heaven, there having been made subject to Him, angels, and authorities, and powers.*

15.

SUFFERING FOR RIGHTEOUSNESS' SAKE, THE ACCOMPANIMENT OF A SEPARATED LIFE (4:1-11)

Verse one

IN 3:18-22 Peter spoke of the sufferings of the Lord Jesus, and of His example of patience and submissiveness under unjust treatment. Now, he exhorts the saints to arm themselves with the same mind that Christ had regarding unjust punishment. Our Lord's attitude toward unjust suffering is found in the words, "It is better, if the will of God be so, that ye suffer for well doing, than for evil doing" (3:17). The Greek word translated "arm yourselves" was used of a Greek soldier putting on his armor and taking his weapons. The noun of the same root was used of a heavy-armed foot-soldier who carried a pike and a large shield. The word was used of heavy-armed as against light-armed troops. Peter could have used the latter word. The Holy Spirit selected the former. The Christian needs the heaviest armor he can get, to withstand the attacks of the enemy of his soul. To have the same attitude toward unjust suffering that the Lord Jesus had, will cause us to react toward this suffering as He did.

The words "suffered in the flesh" are in the same construction as the similar phrase "being put to death in the flesh" (3:18). In the latter expression we found that Peter was speaking of the fact that our Lord was put to death with respect to the flesh, thus suffering with respect to the flesh. This suffering was the result of unjust treatment. The same holds true in 4:1 where the Christian who has suffered in the flesh is the Christian who has suffered ill-treatment from the persecuting world of sinners. The fact that he has been persecuted is an indication of another fact, namely, that he has ceased from sin. The world directs its persecution against those who are living lives of obedience to God, thus those who have ceased from sin. The verb is passive. Literally, the Christian "hath got release" from sin. God broke the power of sin in his life when He saved him. Thus our reaction to unjust suffering should be that of a saint, not a sinner, since we have in salvation been released from sin's compelling power.

Verse two

In this verse, the apostle tells his readers why God breaks the power of the sinful nature at the moment the Christian is saved. It is in order that he should no longer live the rest of his earthly life in the sphere of the cravings (lusts) of men, but live in the sphere of the will of God. The word "lust" in Greek speaks of any strong craving, here, an evil craving.

Verse three

The word "past" describing "time" is in the Greek the perfect participle of a verb meaning "to pass by, to go past." The tense used implies that the course is closed and done, and looked back upon as a standing and accomplished fact. Thus should a Christian view his life previous to salvation, namely, as a closed matter. He died with Christ, and has been raised to newness of life. Old things have passed away. All things have become new. The old habits, associates, practices, places, amusements, everything of the old life which is not in accord with the Word of God should be taboo in the new life he is now living as a Christian. The word "suffice" is in the Greek, "sufficient." That is, Peter argues that there was sufficient time before salvation for the unsaved to go the limit in sin. The word "wrought" means in the Greek "to work out to the end." "Will" is literally, "desire, inclination, counsel," the advice of the world.

Then the apostle enumerates some of the sins which were part of that world out from which they were separated. "Lasciviousness" is the translation of a word which refers to actions that excite disgust and shock public decency. In the New Testament, the prominent idea in the word is that of sensuality. The Greek word translated "lusts" is not limited to the sense of a sexual desire, but has the unrestricted sense of a passionate desire, here a sinful one, as the context indicates. The words "excess of wine" are the translation of a Greek word made of two words, "wine" and "to bubble up or overflow." "Revellings" is the translation of a word which meant at first, "a village merrymaking." Then it came to mean "a carousal" such as a party of revellers parading the streets, or revels held in religious ceremonies, wild, furious, and ecstatic. "Banquetings" is from a Greek word speaking of drinking bouts possibly held in connection with pagan religious rites such as Paul speaks of in I Corinthians 10:14 where he forbids Christians to drink the cup of demons. The Greek word translated "abominable" means "contrary to law and justice, illicit, criminal." These idolatries were forbidden by Roman law. They must have been pretty bad.

Verse four

The word "run" literally means "to run in company with" others. It means here "to run in a troop with others like a band of revellers." The word "excess" is the translation of a Greek word meaning literally "a pouring forth or an overflowing." It was used in classical Greek of the tides which fill the hollows. Alford translates it by the word "slough," a state of moral degradation or spiritual dejection into which one sinks or from which one cannot free one's self. The word "riot" in the Greek text is seen in its classic New Testament usage in Luke 15:13 where the prodigal son squanders his substance with riotous (same word) living. The word is made up of the Greek word meaning "to save" and Alpha privative which makes it mean "not save," and when used as a descriptive word for an individual, speaks of him as being "an abandoned man, an incorrigible," and when used to describe a manner of life, it speaks of "an abandoned dissolute life, profligacy, prodigality." The words "think it strange" do not have the idea in the Greek of thinging something odd or unusual, but of thinking something to be foreign in nature to something else. The people of the world, the former associates of these Christians to whom Peter is writing, thought it a thing foreign to the natures of these Christians when they did not run any more in a troop like a band of revellers with them in the same slough of dissoluteness. They did not realize that their totally depraved nature which before salvation had given them a love for sinful things, now had its power over them broken, and that another nature, the divine nature, had been given them as their new motivating principle of life which caused them to hate the things they once loved and love the things they once hated.

Verse five

The English translation does not make it clear whether the word "who" refers back to the unsaved or to the saved in verse 4. Here is where Greek grammar is an invaluable and accurate help. The word "who" is in apposition with the participle translated "speaking evil," and refers to the people of the world who shall give an account to God who is holding Himself in readiness (Greek) to judge the living ("quick" obsolete English for "living") and the dead.

Verse six

The key to the understanding of this difficult verse is found in the context of the entire book. In 1:6, 7 we are told that the recipients are in heaviness in the midst of manifold trials. In 2:18-25 we have the case of Christian household slaves being unjustly punished because of their Christian testimony. In 3:8-17 the saints are instructed as to their behavior when undergoing persecution. In 4:12-19 the apostle deals with the glory of suffering for righteousness' sake. He speaks of this persecution of the saints by the world as a judgment that begins at the house of God, the Church (4:17). In 4:1-11 he speaks of the necessity of having the mind of Christ as armored protection against the persecution of the world. Thus the phrase "judged according to men," refers to the judgment spoken of in 4:17 which is defined as to its nature by the words in verse 14, "If ye be reproached for the name of Christ."

The words "them that are dead," refer to Christian believers who had died. The gospel had been preached to them and they had become Christians. As a result of this they had been judged according to men while they were on earth. This judgment was in the form of persecution because of their Christian testimony. The word translated "according to" means literally "down," and speaks of domination. This judgment was in the hands of men and was administered by them.

The words "in the flesh" are to be construed with "might be judged," for they balance up the words "in the spirit" which clearly are to be understood with "live." We have here the dative of respect. These Christians were judged with respect to the flesh, that is, with respect to their earthly existence in the body. The natural result of accepting the gospel would be the living of a Christian life, and the natural result of that would be persecution. But these Christians died, many of them as martyrs. Now, in heaven they were living according to the Word of God with respect to their spirits, their human spirits. They in their disembodied state were serving the Lord in the future life.

Verse seven

The word translated "of all things" is first in the sentence, and thus in the emphatic position. "Of all things the end is at hand." "Be ye sober," is literally, "Be ye of sound mind." Sobriety of mind is in view here. "Watch" is the translation of a Greek word meaning "to be calm and collected in spirit." "Unto" is in the Greek literally, "with a view to." Tyndale translates, "That ye may be apt to." That is, a calm and collected spirit is conducive to the act of praying. It results in prayer. The Christian who is always on a tear, whose mind is crowded with fears and worries, who is never at rest in his heart, does not do much praying.

Verse eight

The word "charity" is the translation of the Greek word speaking of God's love (John 3:16), the love produced in our hearts by the Holy Spirit (Rom. 5:5; Gal. 5:22). The word today refers to the act of alleviating the necessities of the poor. The Greek word has no such idea in it. The Greek word here translated "fervent" means literally "stretched out." The idea is that of a love that is extended to reach the one loved. It is the act of one who, instead of living a self-centered life, gives of himself to others. The word means here, "intent, earnest, assiduous." "Have among yourselves" is literally "having (love) toward one another."

The words "above all" are more properly "before all in order of importance." That is, love is a prerequisite to all proper exercises of Christian duty. Courtesy without love is a cold thing. Generosity without love is a harsh thing. Love makes all the other virtues what they should be. The reason for this exhortation to love one another is that love covers a multitude of sins. That is, when one Christian truly loves his fellow Christian, he will not publish abroad his failings, but will cover them up from the sight of others. How much gossip is eliminated when we love each other.

Verse nine

The word "hospitality" is the translation of a Greek word meaning literally "friendly to strangers." Thus the thought in the mind of the apostle is not that of hospitality shown to one's friends who do not need it, but to Christians who in their travels for the Lord Jesus, or for whatever other reason, may be in need of food and shelter. The persecutions which some of these Christians were enduring deprived them often of the necessities of life, and such an exhortation as this was needed.

Verse ten

"As" is in the Greek text "in whatever quality or quantity." The word "gift" here is not the usual Greek word, but one that refers to the special spiritual enablements given graciously to certain Christians as an aid in the discharge of the special duties to which God has called them, as in I Corinthians 12 and 13. The word "stewards" is literally "one who governs a household." It speaks of the responsibility of the proper use and disposition of something entrusted to one's care.

Verse eleven

The Greek word "oracles" was used in classical Greek of the oracular utterances of heathen deities. In the Christian system it refers to divine utterances or revelations.

FULLER TRANSLATION

(1) *Therefore, in view of the fact that Christ suffered with respect to the flesh, you also yourselves put on as armor the same mind, because the one who has suffered with respect to the flesh has gotten release from sin, (2) with a view to his not living the rest of his time while in his physical body in the sphere of the cravings of men, but in the sphere of the will of God. (3) For adequate has been the time that is now past and done with, for you to have carried to its ultimate conclusion the counsel of the Gentiles, walking as you have done in disgusting sensualities, in cravings, in wine-guzzlings, in carousals, in drinking bouts, and in unlawful idolatries,*

(4) *in which they think it a thing alien to you that you do not run in a troop like a band of revellers with them in the same slough of dissoluteness, speaking evil of you,* (5) *who (namely, the people of the world) shall give an account to the One who is holding Himself in readiness to judge the living and the dead.* (6) *For, for this purpose also to the dead was the good news preached, in order that they might be judged by men with respect to their physical existence, but live according to God with respect to their spirit existence.* (7) *But of all things the end has come near. Be of sound mind therefore, and be calm and collected in spirit with a view to (your giving yourselves to) prayer;* (8) *before all things in order of importance, having fervent love among yourselves, because love hides a multitude of sins.* (9) *Show hospitality to one another without murmuring.* (10) *In whatever quality or quantity each one has received a gift, be ministering it among yourselves as good stewards of the variegated grace of God.* (11) *If anyone speaks, as utterances of God let them be. If anyone ministers, let him minister as out of the strength which God supplies, in order that in all things God may be glorified through Jesus Christ, in whom there is the glory and the power forever and ever. Amen.*

16.

THE GLORY OF CHRISTIAN SUFFERING (4:12-19)

Verse twelve

THE word "beloved" is in the Greek, "beloved ones." The word is the Greek word which speaks of God's divine and infinite love. We could translate, "divinely loved ones." Peter uses this word as a descriptive title, reminding the recipients of this letter who were going through much suffering because of persecution, that they were loved with all the love in the heart of God. What a sweet pillow upon which to rest our weary hearts, just to know that our Father loves us. It helps one endure the heartaches and pains of life. The words "think it not strange," are literally "stop thinking it a thing alien" to you. These Christians were thinking that the suffering which they were enduring was a thing foreign or alien to their Christian lives, as if Christianity provided an immunity from suffering. They are exhorted by Peter to think it a natural and expected thing that such suffering for righteousness' sake would come in view of the world's hatred of Christ, and therefore to one who bears His name and reflects Him in his life.

Peter speaks of these sufferings as a fiery trial. The words "fiery trial," are the rendering of a word used also in the Greek translation of the Old Testament in Proverbs 27:21, which word in the A.V. is rendered "a furnace," referring to a smelting furnace where gold is refined. The same word is found in Ps. 66:10 which Vincent translates, "Thou, O God, has proved us: thou hast smelted us, as silver is smelted." The word means literally "a burning," but is used in these passages to refer to a smelting furnace and the smelting process in which gold or silver ore is purified. These sufferings which the recipients of this letter were undergoing constituted the smelting furnace in which their lives were being purified. The words "strange thing" are the translation of a Greek word referring to something alien or foreign in nature. The word "happened" is in the Greek literally "to go together," thus "to happen." But nothing just happens in the life of a Christian. Even this suffering for righteousness' sake is all within His plan. It is used of God to purify our lives from sin.

Verse thirteen

Instead of thinking it a thing alien to them, they are exhorted not only to expect such suffering, but to rejoice in the fact that they can be partakers of Christ's sufferings. The word "inasmuch" is rather "in so far as." That is, the Christian has no cause for rejoicing because of suffering that is brought on because of his own misdoing. But in so far as suffering is the result of doing well, he has cause for rejoicing. His rejoicing arises from the fact that he shares in common with Christ in suffering for righteousness' sake. These sufferings of Christ which we share in common with Him are not His expiatory sufferings on the Cross, but His sufferings for righteousness' sake while enduring the opposition of sinners previous to the Cross. Paul speaks of the same things in Colossians 1:24.

Verse fourteen

In the word "reproached," we have an indication of the character of these sufferings. It was reproach which the world was casting in the teeth of the Christians. Christian suffering in this epistle is limited in its primary application and reference to suffering which is the result of persecution by the world because of one's testimony for the Lord Jesus. A secondary application may be made in the sense that suffering in general, acts as a purifying agency in the life of the Christian when the latter reacts toward it in a meek and submissive way. The Greek word "reproach" is found in Matthew 5:11 where it is translated "revile." The word "if" is the "if" of a fulfilled condition. It could be translated "in view of the fact," or "since." These Christians were being reproached for the name of Christ. This was no hypothetical case.

The apostle says that in view of the fact that they are being reproached, they are happy. The word "happy" is the translation of a Greek word which means "prosperous." It is used in Matthew 5:3-11, where it is translated "blessed." It refers in these contexts to a spiritually prosperous state or condition of the believer. That is, if the world persecutes a Christian, that is an indication of the spiritual prosperity of his life. The world does not persecute a worldly Christian, only a spiritual one. It is spirituality that rubs its fur the wrong way.

But not only is the fact of persecution an indication of a spiritually prosperous life, but also of the fact that the Holy Spirit is resting upon the Christian. The words "rest upon" are the translation of a Greek word used in a manuscript of 103 B.C. as a technical term in agriculture. The writer speaks of a farmer resting his land by sowing light crops upon it. He relieved the land of the necessity of producing heavy crops, and thus gave it an opportunity to recuperate its strength. The word is used in Matthew 11:28 where our Lord says, "Come unto me, all ye that labor and are heavy laden, and I will give you rest," literally, "and I will rest you." Here our Lord causes the sinner who comes to Him to cease from his own efforts at carrying his load of guilt and suffering, taking it upon Himself, allowing the believer in his new life powers to function as a child of God. In our First Peter passage, the Holy Spirit rests and refreshes the believer in the sense that He takes over the saint's battle with sin and the heretofore futile effort at living a life pleasing to God, by giving him victory over the evil nature whose power was broken the moment God saved him, and by producing in his life His own fruit. The Spirit of the Glory, even the Spirit of God, is resting with refreshing power upon the child of

God, causing him to live a life which pleases God and toward
which the world hurls its venom and hate. The words "on
their part he is evil spoken of, but on your part he is glorified," while true, do not appear in the best Greek texts, and
are not therefore thought to be part of the original manuscript that left the hands of Peter. We have therefore not
included them in the translation.

Verse fifteen

The word "suffer" must be taken in its context to mean
"suffer reproach." The form of the original forbids the continuance of an action already going on. Some of the recipients of this letter, before they were saved, had suffered
reproach as murderers, thieves, evildoers, and busybodies.
Peter admonishes them to let these sins be a thing of the
past. What a life many of these had been saved out of. The
word "busybody" means in the Greek, "a self-appointed overseer in other men's matters."

Verse sixteen

The words, "Yet if any man suffer as a Christian" should
be understood in their historical background. The Cult of
the Caesar was the state religion of the Roman empire, in
which the emperor was worshipped as a god. It served two
purposes. The subjects of Rome gave obedience to the laws
of the empire, not only as a political, but as a religious duty.
It also constituted the unifying factor which bound the many
different peoples of the empire into one, and made the military task of holding together its far-flung domain an easier
one. The Greek word for Caesar is *Kaisar*. Those who worshipped the *Kaisar* were called *Kaisarianos*. Christianity
appeared as a rival claimant to world worship and dominion.
The Lord Jesus, the Messiah of Israel, was looked upon in
the Christian Church as the One who would some day come
back and take the government of the world upon His shoul-
der. Those who worshipped Him as God were called

Christianos, worshippers of the Christ as against the *Kaisari-anos,* worshippers of the Caesar. Rome saw that the imperialism of Christianity was challenging the imperialism of the Caesars, and that it was by its propagation, striking at the very vitals of the empire.[1] It answered this by the ten bloody persecutions. It meant and cost something to be a *Christianos* in those days. The members of the Imperial Cult looked down upon and persecuted the members of the Body of Christ. That is what Peter means when he says, "Yet if any man suffer as a Christian, let him not be ashamed." He remembered that awful night when he cowered before the might of Rome and denied his Lord. But Peter the Rock-Man would never do such a thing now. He died a martyr on a Roman cross (John 21:18, 19), tradition tells us, head down, for he would not be crucified as his Lord was.

Verse seventeen

The judgment is the persecution which these saints were undergoing, a disciplinary judgment designed to purify their lives. The word "at" is literally "from." That is, the starting place of the judgment is the Church, and from there as a starting point, the judgment goes on its way to the unsaved.

Verse eighteen

The word "scarcely" is the translation of a Greek word that means literally "with difficulty." The word is used in Acts 14:18 where Paul experienced difficulty in restraining the people at Lystra from sacrificing to him as a god. The context in First Peter speaks of the persecutions which were allowed to come by God as a disciplinary judgment, the purpose of which was to purify their lives. They were being saved with difficulty in the sense that if it was necessary for God to purify the lives of *saints* by these drastic means, namely, persecution and suffering, what can one say as to the position of the *unsaved* in relation to God? If the righteous need disciplinary

---

1. *Bypaths,* pp. 20-32.

judgments, how much more will the unrighteous merit the wrath of God whose offer of righteousness they have rejected.

Verse nineteen

The Greek word "commit" is a banking term meaning "to give in charge as a deposit." Peter exhorts believers who are undergoing persecutions, that in view of the fact that these are allowed to come by God and are designed to purify their lives, they have every reason to trust Him to take care of them through all of their sufferings.

FULLER TRANSLATION

(12) *Divinely loved ones, stop thinking that the smelting process which is (operating) among you and which has come to you for the purpose of testing (you), is a thing alien to you,* (13) *but insofar as you share in common with the sufferings of Christ, be rejoicing, in order that also at the time of the unveiling of His glory, you may rejoice exultingly.* (14) *In view of the fact that you have cast in your teeth as it were, revilings because of the name of Christ, (spiritually) prosperous (are you), because the Spirit of the Glory, even the Spirit of God is resting with refreshing power upon you.* (15) *Now, let no one of you continue to be suffering (reproach) as a murderer or a thief or an evildoer or as a self-appointed overseer in other men's matters.* (16) *But if he suffer (reproach) as a Christian, let him not be ashamed, but let him glorify God because of this name,* (17) *for the time is now, of the judgment beginning at the house of God. But if it start first with us, what shall be the end of those who are not obeying the gospel of God?* (18) *And if he who is righteous is with difficulty being saved, he that is both impious and a sinner, where shall he appear?* (19) *Therefore, also let those who are suffering according to the will of God, commit the safekeeping of their souls by a continuance in the doing of good, to a faithful Creator.*

17.

THE RESPONSIBILITIES OF ELDERS (5:1-5a)

Verse one

THE Greek word "elder" was used as a designation of a man advanced in years. It became one of the official designations of an officer in a local church who in other places is called an overseer or a bishop (Acts 20:17, 28; I Tim. 3:2), and whose duty it was to exercise spiritual oversight and authority over its members. The Greek for "who am also an elder" could also be rendered "who am a fellow-elder," which is decisive against the primacy of Peter. Peter neither claimed nor assumed any higher position than that of an ordinary elder in the Church. The word "witness" is the translation of the Greek word from which we get our word "martyr." It does not refer to the act of seeing, but to the act of testifying to what one has seen. Peter is not merely claiming to have seen the crucifixion, but to have been retained to give testimony concerning what he had seen. In II Peter 1:16, the apostle uses another word which is translated "eyewitnesses." There he refers to the fact of his having seen the incidents in our Lord's life. But in 5:1 he speaks of himself as an official witness called to testify by God.

Verse two

The word "feed" is the translation of a Greek word which literally means "to shepherd," and includes the duties of a shepherd, tending, feeding, guiding, and guarding the flock of God. The noun form of the word is translated "pastors" in Ephesians 4:11. The word "oversight" is the translation of the same Greek word in another form which in other places is rendered by the words "overseer," or "bishop," referring to the spiritual care of the flock. The words "filthy lucre" are literally in the Greek text "base or dishonorable gain." The pastor is not to commercialize his ministry.

Verse three

The words "being lords over" in the Greek text speak of a high-handed autocratic rule over the flock, which is forbidden a true shepherd. One could translate, "lording it over." However, this does not do away with a God-ordained, properly exercised authority which should be administered in the local church by the pastor and the elders. Paul speaks of this in I Thessalonians 5:12 and I Timothy 5:17, using another Greek word. The word "heritage" is the translation of a word meaning "a lot" as in the words, "gave forth their lots" (Acts 1:26). Here it refers to the lots or charges given the elders. Alford translates, "the portions entrusted to you." It is interesting to note that our word "cleric" comes from this Greek word, and that the latter was contracted to "clerk," which in ecclesiastical writings referred to a pastor of a church. Instead of lording it over those portions of God's flock assigned to them, these local pastors are exhorted to be an ensample to the entire flock. The word translated "ensample" means "a print left as an impression after a blow has been struck, a pattern or model of something else." Under-shepherds should be living patterns or models of the Chief Shepherd, the Lord Jesus.

Verse four

The Greek word translated "crown" referred to a crown of victory in the Greek athletic games, a crown given for military valor, or a festal garland worn at marriage feasts.[1] Here it is the reward given to faithful shepherds of the flock of God. "Fadeth" is a participle in the Greek describing this crown. The word in its noun form was the name of a flower

1. *Bypaths*, pp. 60-70.

that did not wither or fade, and which when picked, revived in water. The crown given to victors in either athletics or war was made of oak or ivy leaves, the festal garlands of the marriage feast, of flowers. These would wither and fade. But the victor's crown which the Lord Jesus will give His faithful under-shepherds will never wither or fade. What form this reward will take, is not stated. Paul says that his crown of rejoicing at the coming of the Lord Jesus for His Church will be made of the souls he won (I Thess. 2:19).

Verse five a

The word "younger" is in this context not to be interpreted primarily as referring to the younger element in the church as composed merely of individuals, but as organized into guilds or associations. Inscriptions speak of youth organizations in the Greek cities of Asia Minor. The idea could easily have been taken over into the local church. The word "elders" in this context does not refer to the older men as a class, but to the elders of the local church as a group. It would seem therefore that the word "younger" would refer, not to the younger element as such, but to organizations composed of younger people. These organizations are exhorted to be in obedience to the elders of the church.

FULLER TRANSLATION

(1) *Elders therefore who are among you, I exhort, I who am your fellow-elder, and one who saw the sufferings of Christ and who has been retained as a witness to bear testimony concerning them, who also am a fellow-partaker of the glory which is about to be unveiled;* (2) *shepherd the flock of God among you, doing so not by reason of constraint put upon you, but willingly according to God; nor yet as lording it in a high-handed manner over the portions of the flock assigned to you, but as becoming patterns for the flock.* (4) *And when the Chief Shepherd appears, you shall receive the conqueror's unfading crown of glory.* (5) *Likewise, younger ones, be in subjection to the elders.*

18.

CHRISTIAN HUMILITY, A SAFEGUARD AGAINST SATAN AND A SOURCE OF STRENGTH IN SUFFERING (5:5b-14)

Verse five b

THE subject of humility begins with the second sentence of verse five. The words "be subject to" are not in the best Greek texts. We have left them out of the fuller translation. "Be clothed with" is the translation of a word which speaks of the act of tying or tucking up the long outer garments of the oriental around the waist as a roll or band or girth. It refers to the same action as Peter mentions in 1:13 where he says, "Gird up the loins of your mind." The word in its noun form referred to a slave's apron under which the loose outer garments were gathered. The exhortation is to put on humility as a working virtue which would make all the other virtues what they should be, thus workable in the Christian scheme of things. The other virtues such as kindness, generosity, justice, goodness, longsuffering, when saturated with humility, are most acceptable and praiseworthy, but when seen in a proud person, are like clanging brass or a tinkling cymbal.

The word "resisteth" in the Greek is a military term, used of an army drawn up for battle. Pride calls out God's armies. God sets Himself in array against the proud person. The word "proud" is the translation of a Greek word which means literally "to show above," and thus describes the proud person as one who shows himself above others. The word "humble" is the translation of the Greek word rendered "lowly" in Matthew 11:29, where it describes our Lord's character. The word is found in an early secular document where it speaks

of the Nile River in its low stage in the words, "It runs low."
The word means "not rising far from the ground." It describes the Christian who follows in the humble and lowly
steps of his Lord.

Verse six

The verb translated "humble yourselves" is not in the
aorist middle but the passive voice, which means that the
subject of the verb is passive in the hands of God and is
acted upon by Him. The exhortation is, "Be humbled," or
"Suffer yourselves to be humbled." The humbling process
which God was using was the persecution and suffering
through which these Christians were passing. Peter exhorts
these believers to react towards these in a God-honoring way,
to be submissive to the discipline which God was using to
make them more humble. But with this exhortation comes
also a note of comfort and hope in that the presence of
humility in the life of a Christian is the prerequisite that God
demands before He will exalt that Christian to a high place
of privilege and honor in His service. As someone has said,
"He must take a low place before God, who would take a
high place before men."

Verse seven

Then comes an exhortation to cast all our care upon Him.
The command is directly and vitally related to the context.
These Christians were undergoing such persecution that the
circumstances in which they found themselves gave abundant
opportunity for that sin called worry. The apostle exhorts
them that while this humbling process is going on, they
should cast all their care upon God. The word "care" is the
translation of a Greek word which means "anxiety" or
"worry." The word "all" in the Greek text has the idea, not
of every worry that comes along, but the whole of their
worries. They are to cast upon God the whole of their worries, that is, come to the place where they resolve to cast the

whole of their future worries upon Him, and the result will be that when those things that would otherwise worry them come up, they will not worry. The word "cast" is the translation of a word that means "having deposited with." It refers here to a direct and once-for-all committal to God of all that would give us concern. The words "for he careth for you" can be translated literally, "for it is a care to Him concerning you," or "for you are His concern." Anxiety is a self-contradiction to true humility. Unbelief is, in a sense, an exalting of self against God in that one is depending upon self and failing to trust God. Why worry therefore, if we are His concern. He is more concerned about our welfare than we could possibly be. Furthermore, since the humbling process has been allowed to come to us in the permissive will of God, and He is using it to accomplish His purpose in our lives, He has it under His control and us in His care. In it all He is concerned about us, therefore, again, why worry?[1]

Verse eight

In the words "be sober" sobriety of mind is enjoined. "Be mentally self-controlled," is the idea. The words "be vigilant" in the Greek present the idea of "be awake and watchful." The word "adversary" is the translation of a word used of an opponent in a lawsuit. The word "devil" is the word used in the English translation for *diabolos* which comes from a word *diaballo* which means literally, "to throw over or across, to send over." It was used in classical Greek with the meanings, "to traduce, calumniate, slander, accuse, defame," and was used not only of those who bring a false charge against one, but also of those who disseminate the truth concerning a man and do so maliciously, insidiously, with hostility. All that, the devil is in his character and in his actions against the saints. The word "roaring" in the Greek text speaks of the howl of a beast in fierce hunger.

---

1. *Nuggets*, pp. 43, 44.

Verse nine

The Greek word translated "resist" means "to withstand, to be firm against someone else's onset" rather than "to strive against that one." The Christian would do well to remember that he cannot fight the devil. The latter was originally the most powerful and wise angel God created. He still retains much of that power and wisdom as a glance down the pages of history and a look about one today will easily show. While the Christian cannot take the offensive against Satan, yet he can stand his ground in the face of his attacks. Cowardice never wins against Satan, only courage.

The word "stedfast" is a military term. Paul uses it in Colossians 2:3 when he says "beholding your order," that is, "beholding your solid front or close phalanx." The Greek phalanx was a body of heavy-armed infantry formed in ranks and files close and deep. Pope has a line, "The Grecian phalanx, moveless as a tower." The word speaks of solidity in the very mass and body of the thing itself. The exhortation is most appropriate to Peter whose name means "A Rock." He was that at Pentecost and after, for the Holy Spirit controlled him. Any saint today can be the same, and by the energy of that same Spirit. The words "in the faith" refer to the believer's own faith, the definite article here pointing to ownership. That is, the Christian is to stand firm against the onset of the devil, not in himself, but in the exercise of a faith that depends upon the strengthening and protecting power of God.

Verse ten

The phrase "the God of all grace" speaks of God as the source of all spiritual comfort and help for every occasion. The word translated "unto" means literally "with a view to." The word "called" in its Greek usage means more than an invitation. It is a divine summons. The one summoned is constituted willing to obey the summons, not against but with his free will and accord. It is an effectual call. The one called always responds through the enablement of the Holy Spirit. This effectual call is with a view to God's eternal glory. That is, God calls us into salvation in order that He may derive glory for Himself by virtue of our being saved. He who has called us in His grace will supply all needed grace until we are ushered into the Glory. God's eternal glory is involved in His keeping a believer in salvation. Thus we see the eternal security of the Christian. The words "by Christ Jesus" are to be construed with the word "called." Christ Jesus is the sphere in which that calling takes place. That is, in order that God might call sinners with a view to His eternal glory, they need to be saved, and salvation is found only in the Lord Jesus. Therefore, this calling is in the sphere of or within the scope of the Saviour's saving power and work.

The words "a while" in the Greek text are literally "a little while." The rest of the verse is not a wish nor a petition but a prediction. The verbs are all in the future tense. The words "make you perfect" are not the translation of the Greek word *teleioo* which means "to perfect"[1] in the sense of "to make spiritually mature and complete," but from a word meaning "to fit or join together." The predominating idea in the verb is adjustment, the putting of parts into right relationship and connection with one another. It is the same word translated "perfecting" in Ephesians 4:12, where the gifted servants of the Lord mentioned were given to the Church for the equipping of the saints for ministering work.[2] The word was used of James and John mending their nets, thus equipping them for service (Mark 1:19). Here the word refers to God mending the lives of Christians, thus equipping them for usefulness in His service. The word in First Peter speaks of the work of the Holy Spirit in rounding out the spiritual life of the saint so that he is equipped for both the living of a Christian life and the service of the Lord Jesus.

1. *Treasures*, pp. 113-121.
2. *Nuggets*, pp. 35-37.

The word "stablish" is the translation of a Greek word whose root is akin to the word translated "stedfast" in 5:9. It speaks of a solid foundational position. Alford translates, "shall ground you as on a foundation." Bengel has a helpful note on this verse; "Shall perfect, that no defect remain in you, shall stablish that nothing may shake you, shall strengthen that you may overcome every adverse force." No comments on verse eleven.

Verse twelve

In verses 12-14 we probably have the postscript in Peter's own handwriting. This would indicate that Silvanus was the amanuensis, the one to whom Peter dictated the letter and by whom it was sent. The word "faithful" is preceded by the definite article in the Greek text, showing that he was well-known to the recipients. The English word "suppose" might suggest that Peter was not sure of the character of Silvanus. But the Greek word denotes a settled persuasion or assurance. It indicates that the apostle's judgment of Silvanus was given as a recommendation. Robertson translates "as I account him." The word "stand" is imperative in the Greek text, "in which stand."

Verse thirteen

There is a division of opinion among commentators as to whether Peter is using the name "Babylon" in its apocalyptic sense of Rome, or whether he is referring here to the literal city on the Euphrates. It would seem that he is referring to the city of Babylon itself, from the following considerations. First, the fact that the word is used in a mystical sense in the Book of The Revelation, which book makes use of such figures, is no argument for the mystical use of the word in a writing of a different character. Second, the other geographical references in First Peter have undoubtedly the literal meaning, and it would be natural to expect that Peter's use of the name "Babylon" would be literal also. Third, there is no reason to suppose that when this epistle was written the city of Rome was currently known among Christians as Babylon. Fourth, The Revelation was written after the composition of Peter's letter, and therefore he could not be following John's use of the name. Fifth, wherever the city of Rome is mentioned in the New Testament, with the single exception of The Revelation (and even there it is distinguished as "Babylon the Great"), it gets its usual name, Rome. Sixth, there is very good ground for believing that at the date of the writing of Peter's letter the Jewish, and also the pagan population of the city and its vicinity, was very considerable.

The words "Greet one another with a kiss of love" refer to a custom in the early Church when after prayers, the brethren welcomed each other with a kiss. Chrysostom calls it "the peace by which the Apostle expels all disturbing thought and beginning of small-mindedness . . . this kiss softens and levels." The practice was liable to abuse as Clement of Alexandria shows when he says, "love is judged not in a kiss but in good will. Some do nothing but fill the church with noise of kissing. There is another — an impure — kiss full of venom pretending to holiness." Therefore the practice was regulated, men kissed men only, and the custom gradually dwindled.

FULLER TRANSLATION

(5b) *Moreover, all of you, bind about yourselves as a girdle, humility toward one another, because God opposes Himself to those who set themselves above others, but gives grace to those who are lowly.* (6) *Suffer yourselves therefore to be humbled under the mighty hand of God, in order that you He may exalt in due time,* (7) *having deposited with Him once for all the whole of your worry, because to Him it is a matter of concern respecting you.* (8) *Be of a sober mind, be watchful. Your adversary who is a slanderer, namely, the devil, as a lion roaring in fierce hunger, is constantly walking about, always seeking someone to be devouring. (9) Stand immovable against his onset, solid as a rock in your faith, knowing that the same kind of sufferings are being accomplished in your brotherhood which is in the world. (10) But the God of every grace, the One who has called you in Christ with a view to His eternal glory, after you have suffered a little while, shall Himself perfect you, shall establish you firmly, shall strengthen you, shall ground you as on a foundation. (11) To Him let there be ascribed this power forever and forever, Amen. (12) Through Silvanus, the faithful brother, which is my estimate of him, briefly I have written to you, exhorting and testifying that this is the true grace of God, in which stand. (13) The (church) in Babylon, elect with you, sends greeting, also Mark my son. (14) Greet one another with a kiss of love. Peace be with you all who are in Christ.*

INDEX